942

CLIENT
CONFIDENTIAL

Seán Hartnett joined the British Army in 1998 and served for almost seven years before moving first to South Africa, then Australia and finally returning to Ireland just as the Celtic Tiger was collapsing. He has worked as a security consultant for major companies and on government projects worldwide. He has also worked in the area of commercial espionage and counter espionage. His first book, *Charlie One*, was published by Merrion Press in 2016.

CLIENT CONFIDENTIAL

SPOOKS, SECRETS AND COUNTER-ESPIONAGE DURING THE CELTIC TIGER

SEÁN HARTNETT

MERRION
PRESS

First published in 2019 by
Merrion Press
An imprint of Irish Academic Press
10 George's Street
Newbridge
Co. Kildare
Ireland
www.merrionpress.ie

9781785372100 (Paper)
9781785372117 (Kindle)
9781785372124 (Epub)
9781785372131 (PDF)

British Library Cataloguing in Publication Data
An entry can be found on request

Library of Congress Cataloging in Publication Data
An entry can be found on request

Typeset in Minion Pro 12/15 pt

Cover design by Jeffers & Sons, Belfast.

Printed and bound by TJ International, Padstow, Cornwall

'Behind every successful fortune there is a crime.'

— Mario Puzo, *The Godfather*

Contents

Some of the sensitive discoveries made by the author during TSCM sweeps have not been disclosed for legal reasons. For security reasons, some of the names, locations and dates have been changed.

Glossary

ADC	Aide-de-camp
Bakkie	South African open-backed utility vehicle
CAB	Criminal Assets Bureau
CEO	Chief Executive Officer
CFD	Contracts for Difference
CFO	Chief Financial Officer
DDDA	Dublin Docklands Development Authority
DSO	Director Special Operations
EPA	Environmental Protection Agency
HFO	Heavy Fuel Oil
ILP	Irish Life and Permanent
InfoSec	Information Security
IPMS	In-Place Monitoring System
IPS	Irish Prison Service
IRFU	Irish Rugby Football Union
JCU-NI	Joint Communications Unit – Northern Ireland
NCC	National Conference Centre
NLJD	Non-Linear Junction Detector
OP	Observation Post
OSG	Operational Support Group
OSU	Operational Support Unit
PABX	Private Automatic Branch Exchange
PIRA	Provisional Irish Republican Army
PPP	Public–private partnership
PSNI	Police Service Northern Ireland
PTZ	Pan Tilt Zoom
RF	Radio Frequency
RIRA	Real Irish Republican Army
TSCM	Technical Surveillance Countermeasures
VCP	Vehicle Check Point

Prologue

It was almost midnight and I had been sitting in a parked van on St Stephen's Green, Dublin, for over three hours. I had hired the van a few days earlier, kitted it out with roof ladders and thrown some tools in the back. I never used my own personal vehicles on jobs like this. It was disguised as just another building-services vehicle, one of the tens of thousands roaming around the country, thanks to the development book of the Celtic Tiger. The only break I had taken was a walk around the Green, not to stretch my legs but to scan for the tell-tale signs of somebody watching either me or the building I was about to enter.

There was no indication of any suspect vehicle, nor were there any eyes lingering on me for longer than they should have. Taxi drivers and the last of the late-night revellers were all that remained on the streets that night. I had paid a few random visits to the Green over the previous three days, trying to spot any surveillance on the building, but there had been no obvious sign of a mobile-listening post within an operational distance of the building. Of course, there may have been a static post set up in one of the adjacent buildings, hence my visit tonight. I sat across the street at an angle from the entrance to the building, using my mirrors to keep an eye on the doorway and the approaches to it. Satisfied that I was alone, I got out of the van and started to unload the necessary kit. A toolbox, a stepladder and two flight cases contained everything I would require, but it was a struggle to get them to the door in one trip. I had no intentions of making a second trip – the less that was seen of me, the better.

PROLOGUE

It was a bitterly cold night, which was the perfect excuse to be wearing a hooded jacket and gloves, but the weather wasn't the reason I had those on. The hood would prevent any CCTV surveillance cameras from identifying me as I entered the building, and the gloves hid the pair of latex gloves I was wearing beneath them, ensuring I would leave no fingerprints behind. I got to the entrance, carefully keeping my head down, and then used the key and the pass card that had been supplied to me to enter the building. It was a dark winter night in early 2007, and I had just entered the headquarters of Anglo Irish Bank. Time to get to work!

Chapter 1

From the Seaside to the Bogside

There was still one active surveillance device in the room. I knew it was there because the sophisticated scanner I had running – the only piece of technology I was allowed that day – was showing one last active signal. It was almost twelve hours since I had started, and I had already located five separate covert devices in the boardroom I was working in, each one more elaborately hidden than the previous. The final bug had eluded me for almost four hours, and I was under pressure. The sweat stung my eyes and I was covered from head to toe in dust, dirt and cobwebs. The fingertip search I had been carrying out since early morning had seen me crawling through ceiling spaces, removing floor tiles and turning over every item in the room.

The search would have been over hours ago had I been allowed to use the handheld electronic search equipment designed specifically for this type of situation, but they were purposely denied to me. I looked around the room again trying to put myself in the position of the person who had planted the device, just as we had been taught to do over the last week. Where would I have put it? What looked out of place? It was then I spotted the slightly frayed stitching on one of the six office chairs around the boardroom table. I knelt before the chair, carefully scanning the fabric, and there it was: the tiniest of pinholes. I removed the Stanley knife from my tool belt and cut along the stitching, careful not to damage the fabric of the chair. There was no doubt the chair had been tampered with; the stuffing came out far too easily. After a gentle probe, a small battery-powered transmitter appeared, followed by the tiny microphone. Result!

I emerged into the courtyard of the training facility located not far from Portsmouth, my tired eyes squinting in the summer evening sunshine. This unassuming facility was the training ground for some of the most advanced surveillance and counter-surveillance training courses in the world. The instructor approached, and I knew from the look on his face that he wasn't too pleased.

'Too slow on that last one, Hartnett. You should have picked that device up on the first sweep and when you didn't, you ignored those chairs second time around. Check and double-check! You won't have twelve hours on a live job.'

It was the penultimate day of the Technical Surveillance Countermeasures (TSCM) course, and the following day would be the final written and practical exam. Throughout the last two weeks, we had been taught the principles of TSCM, understanding radio frequency (RF) propagation, mains-powered surveillance devices and methods of disguising eavesdropping devices. More importantly, we had been shown the practical skills of carrying out a physical TSCM search and what made a good sweep team.

While all the vulnerabilities to covert surveillance and the vast array of commercial surveillance and counter-surveillance tools were covered on the course, it was the ability to find devices with just a physical search that was at the heart of our training. The practical search exercises had proved increasingly difficult, but it was the 'how' and 'why' of telephone taps and the various ways that surveillance devices could be hidden in everyday items that fascinated me. The training here was second to none.

I would have to be sharper tomorrow. If I passed this TSCM course, I would be a fully certified security consultant, perfect for my planned move back to 'civvy street' from the military. I had already amassed a whole raft of qualifications during my career to date. My masterclass in CCTV, which covered the A–Z of closed-circuit television from an enhanced technical perspective, was devised to develop skills in design, consultancy and commissioning of CCTV systems, but I was using it mainly to develop covert CCTV surveillance networks.

While video evidence, confidentiality, human rights, law and legal issues associated with covert CCTV were all covered, they would prove to be of little concern in my current line of work. My immediate job requirements were more focused on building and utilising practical covert hides, encrypted transmission systems and getting covert pictures from A to B. I had been on other courses at this same facility: Intruder Alarm Installation and Access Control courses didn't benefit me in the installation of such systems but helped to defeat them. The ability to bypass security and surveillance systems allowed for the opportunity to install covert listening devices and cameras in operationally sensitive areas. The next day I sat and passed my final exams before embarking on a journey that would lead to a life of surveillance and counter-surveillance in the world of commercial espionage.

My interest in surveillance and counter-surveillance stemmed from my military career with the British army. I joined after leaving university in 1998. It was the best move I ever made, and I stand by that decision to this day. I grew up in a small village on the south coast of Ireland and, in truth, I couldn't wait to leave the place. Life at home was far from happy, and I took the first opportunity to get away. This came in the form of a place at university to study science. By the second year of my degree, I knew that working in a laboratory for the rest of my days wasn't for me. I yearned for some adventure and travel, and the British army would offer me both.

My family had strong republican ties, so my decision to join the British army came as somewhat of a shock. In reality, the leap wasn't that great, as my father had served in the RAF and my grandfather in the British army. I was just carrying on a tradition of military service. The selection process took about a year, but soon I found myself at Palace Barracks in Belfast swearing an oath to the Queen. Any momentary discomfort quickly passed as I was bundled on a flight to England to begin my military training.

I was trained as a telecommunications engineer at the Royal School of Signals. There, I learned to repair some of the most advanced telecommunications equipment on the planet, including the holy grail: military encryption systems. After almost eighteen months of training, I was transferred to my first operational unit in Wales, where I specialised in Electronic Warfare. This involved everything from direction-finding equipment, intercept units and, most importantly of all, communications-jamming equipment. From there I was lucky enough to complete tours of duty in Sierra Leone, during its brutal civil war, and Oman, as part of one of the largest joint exercises conducted by the British military since the Falklands War. My final posting would be to Northern Ireland. To say it was an eye-opener would be an understatement. Nothing is as it appears in Northern Ireland, and I learned that first-hand. It changed my perceptions of both the military and political landscape there forever. My first book, *Charlie One*, was an exposé the British MOD hoped would never be told.

My military career was going well. I was now a sergeant, but the arduous tours of duty in Sierra Leone and Northern Ireland had taken their toll, and I felt it was time to call it a day. My partner and I decided to return to her home country of South Africa to start afresh. Life in the military teaches you the ability to pack up and move quickly, and no sooner was the house in the UK sold, we were off to South Africa. I was excited about the move: a new country, a new house and a career in the security industry built on my military experience. We moved to South Africa's Garden Route, to the marina town of Knysna. Nothing could have been more idyllic: a picture-perfect lagoon sheltered by the spectacular Knysna heads. It was how I had always pictured paradise. However, this postcard image hid a mass of poverty, crime and corruption. The abolishment of apartheid and the introduction of affirmative action had not delivered the socio-economic reforms that had been promised; in truth, much of the black community in South Africa were worse off than they had ever been. This led to an explosion in crime, so security was not seen as a luxury but as a necessity.

Sometimes people are given to exaggeration, but I can't emphasise enough how dangerous South Africa can be. The following are just some of the crime figures for South Africa for 2004/2005 (from Crime Stats SA):

- Murder: 18,793

- Attempted Murder: 24,516

- GBH (grievous bodily harm): 249,369

- Sexual Offences: 69,117

- Street Robbery: 100,436

- Residential Robbery: 276,164

- Non-Residential Robbery: 56,048

- Carjacking: 12,434

- Vehicle Theft: 83,857

- Vehicle Break-Ins: 148,512

- Common Robbery: 90,825

- Common Assault: 267,857

- Illegal Possession of Firearms: 15,497

But every cloud has a silver lining, and the figures above resulted in an almost insurmountable amount of work for those working within the security industry in South Africa, myself included.

Security in South Africa is very different to that in Ireland; an intruder alarm system is simply not enough. The perimeter of most houses and housing complexes is guarded by electric fences with enough voltage to cook someone. Doors and windows are protected not only by the typical electronic sensors, but with additional gates and steel bars. Panic alarms are found all over homes in South Africa, and once one is activated, a heavily armed security patrol is immediately dispatched to the premises. These patrols do not hold back; they shoot first and ask questions later. Finally, as if all these other security precautions are not enough, most South African property owners have firearms permits. Despite all of this, home invasions and robberies continued to soar, driven by the extreme poverty in the country – a situation no government to date has been able to successfully address.

I could have worked 24/7 had I wished. The money was good, and the living was easy. We were establishing ourselves well in Knysna, making good friends and a nice home, but something was missing. I was bored. I missed the excitement of the bad old days in the military, the hectic pace of it all, and yes, even the pressure of the high-intensity operations that we carried out. The 9 mm Sig Sauer pistol that I had purchased, which was now almost permanently tucked into my waistband, only reminded me further of the life I was missing. The adage from my old army boss of 'better to be judged by twelve than carried by six' was always there in the back of my mind.

Thankfully, all that was about to change. The opportunity to utilise my old skills and experience in surveillance was about to come my way. I had no idea that the job would lead to such a high-profile investigation and ultimate arrest.

Chapter 2

The Scorpion's Sting

The Scorpions swooped on former deputy president Jacob Zuma's luxury home at 6 a.m. on Thursday, as well as on Schabir Shaik's home in Durban and other premises around the country in a massive raid. The Scorpions had warrants related to the forthcoming State versus Jacob Zuma case and said they were looking for faxes, records of gifts, correspondence – in short, any material that might relate to the trial of Zuma on charges of corruption. Raids were also conducted on the Pretoria home and offices of Pierre Moynot – Managing Director of Thint, the African arm of Thomson International – the arms dealer found by the Durban court to have been involved in Shaik's attempt to arrange a bribe for Zuma. Also raided on Thursday morning were the offices of Mike Hulley, Zuma's Durban attorney.

I stood staring at the TV screen as the reporter continued with her broadcast. The raid had been conducted at Zuma's home on Epping Road, Johannesburg. It was 18 August

2005, just a couple of months after I had completed the surveillance vehicle fit-out job for 'Tommy'.

I had no idea who I was meeting, only that it was at the request of my friend, Villi. No further information had been offered. It was I who had chosen the meeting place, the East Head Café, high up on the Knysna heads overlooking the entrance to the beautiful Knysna lagoon. I had picked it for a good reason: the outdoor seating area was exposed to the winds blowing over the top of the heads from the ocean, making eavesdropping, either human or electronic, very difficult. While I trusted Villi, I also knew he had a very shady background, especially from the days of apartheid. He had been heavily involved in the smuggling in of vehicles and their parts, and the smuggling out of diamonds during the period of international embargoes. I also knew he had friends in the South African police, but I wasn't sure which part of his social circle I was about to sit down with.

I had arrived early, taking a spot at the furthest end of the outdoor café, closest to the water, giving me a perfect view of the entrance. It helped that I knew the owners well, so was perfectly at ease in my surroundings. As soon as the guy walked through the ivy-covered archway I knew he was the one I was meeting. Apart from the slight bulge at his waistband, indicating he was carrying a weapon (nothing unusual in SA), and another bulge on his left hip showing he was carrying spare magazines, this guy oozed government services, either military or police. It was in his bearing, the confident way in which he moved, his eyes scanning and then evaluating the surroundings in one fluid movement. One of the hardest things for covert surveillance operators to do is to disguise any former military or law enforcement background they might have. It takes years of practice to shake loose and even then, to the trained eye, it is easy to spot. He must have pinged me just as quickly because he strode directly over to my table and took a seat opposite me without introduction. His features were average in every way – the grey man, nothing extraordinary about him. Time to find out what the hell this was all about.

One of my favourite things about South Africans is their ability to get straight to the point, no mindless waffle.

'Villi says you know a bit about the tech side of surveillance?' he said, before asking the waitress for a Castle beer.

'A bit,' I replied, somewhat cagily. After all, I still didn't know if this guy was planning a bona fide surveillance operation or a bank heist.

'I've got a job coming up. Need eyes on a target, 24/7.'

He must have seen the hesitation in my eyes, the hundred questions passing through my mind in those few split seconds.

'In or out?' he asked, abruptly.

To be honest, I knew the answer as soon as I had agreed to meet this guy, regardless of what side of the law the job was on. 'I'm in,' I replied, and a broad grin spread across my face.

I then donned the mantle of a covert surveillance technician. I needed details and lots of them. For the next two hours I fired question after question at him: static or mobile target? How close can we get vehicles to the target? Duration of the operation? Will he need a body-worn kit for operators on the ground and remote viewing and control of the cameras? Is there high ground overlooking the target? Do we have access to local telecommunications masts? Will there be cooperation with local law enforcement? (This would indicate who I might actually be working for.) How long until the operation goes live? And finally, what was the budget for the operation?

No doubt this guy was a thorough professional, as this wasn't his first rodeo. He did his best to answer my questions, but there were huge holes in the intelligence I was being given. Nothing new there – it was just like the old days in Northern Ireland, and I had no doubt it was being withheld intentionally. There was no mention of the name of the target, and I wasn't naïve enough to ask such a stupid question, but a picture was building in my mind. While the target would be both static and mobile, I was only to worry about the static side of things. This told me they were using covert operators on the ground for the mobile work. This was a security forces job then. I didn't know which agency was involved yet, but that didn't matter. At least it was a legitimate operation. The target had their own professional security detail. Great! Operational security was going to be a huge issue. Getting the covert surveillance assets in and out of the target area would have to be carefully orchestrated.

The word 'professional' told me that the target was no ordinary run-of-the-mill criminal. It was either a major figure in organised crime or a corrupt official. My interest was piqued. The duration of the operation was indefinite, which dictated how long each surveillance vehicle could be left in place before needing to be replaced by another. Despite what the Hollywood movies portray, surveillance vehicles cannot be left in place indefinitely to keep eyes on a target. The batteries supplying the kit would run down, and if you keep the engine ticking over, you draw unwanted attention to yourself. So, I was going to need multiple vehicles with at least one overwatch camera – not easy with a security detail keeping a watchful eye. The surveillance cameras would need to be viewed remotely from a distant control room, and, even more challenging, they would need to be fully controllable from that location. There would be no cooperation from local police units, but there would be full access to all their intelligence, along with details of their patrol patterns and timings. That was it. This was an intelligence unit operating without the knowledge of the local police force. The realisation must have shown on my face.

'We are keeping this operation tight. We can't use any of our normal support units. Operational security is a must. We are worried about leaks, both to the target and the media,' he said.

I wanted to know more, but that would be it for the day. I hastily scribbled down a list of further information I would need: maps of the area, equipment that would be available to me, and most important of all, the cameras and vehicles that I wanted for the job. We arranged to meet the following day at one of the many industrial units that Villi owned in a place called Mossel Bay, about a ninety-minute drive from Knysna.

As he got up to leave, he stuck his hand out to offer a handshake. 'Tommy's the name,' he said.

I took his hand and gave it a firm shake. 'My arse it is!' I replied, and both of us chuckled knowingly.

'Two weeks off? Where are we going?' She was fully expecting me to name some luxury resort or cosmopolitan city, but once more Steff, my partner of several years, was about to be disappointed.

'It's not a vacation. I'm taking on a job. Just a couple of weeks and I'll be done. It will be some extra money, and we'll use it to take a proper holiday later in the year.'

It was the evening of my meeting at the East Head Café, and I was trying to be honest and upfront. I could see her expression was one of sadness, not because we weren't going on holiday, but because I was returning to the life that had caused us so much stress in the past. I kept the details deliberately vague, not that Steff had ever asked any probing questions before.

'Is it dangerous?' she asked, quietly.

'Not in the slightest,' I quickly replied. It was a fair assumption. As far as I could tell, I would be fitting some kit out and that would be it. Unlike the tours of duty I had been on in the army, this would be a walk in the park.

'I'm not going back to that life. This one, and this one only,' she stated through gritted teeth.

I agreed, but even as the words left my mouth, I knew it was a lie; this wouldn't be my last covert job.

I drove to Mossel Bay the next morning. The sun was only just rising above the heads as I left Knysna. It was breathtaking as always. The industrial unit was one of hundreds located near the port. It was a small compound containing a number of garages and surrounded by a high fence. All the usual security measures that any commercial unit in South Africa would have – electric fence and alarm system – were all visible, but oddly there was no CCTV system. No one wanted any recordings of what was going on here or who was coming and going.

'Tommy' was there to meet me, accompanied by two of his colleagues. No introductions were made. He had all the information I had requested at the previous meeting, but it didn't make for great reading. The maps showed the location of the target house – a premises in the upmarket Epping Road, Forest Town area of Johannesburg. Residential locations always posed certain problems: people are naturally nosy and notice anything unusual in their neighbourhood, strange vehicles in particular. Worse still was the lack of a suitable communications mast or public buildings that could be used to mount both an overwatch camera and a microwave link back to the control room. The scenic, tree-lined avenue created another problem: trees interfere with both radio and microwave signals. Maybe this wasn't going to be plain sailing after all.

'Could we piggyback onto the local police network?' I asked Tommy.

'Not an option, I'm afraid. OPSEC [Operational Security] dictates that the team is kept small and compartmentalised,' he replied.

It was time to take a look at what surveillance kit would be available to me. It wasn't much, certainly not to the standard I had when working on intelligence operations for the British, but it would have to do. I had been taught to build my own surveillance cameras from component level when needs be, so I would cannibalise what was here to make what I really needed. Next, I took a look at the three vehicles I had asked for: a bakkie (a Southern African open-back utility vehicle) of which there were tens of thousands in Johannesburg; a VW Jetta, and finally something with a bit of style, a Mercedes. All three would fit into the upmarket neighbourhood where the target lived: the bakkie would be disguised as a landscaping vehicle; the VW Jetta as a housewife's car and the Merc, well that wouldn't raise any eyebrows given the prestigious nature of the area.

I decided to start with the VW Jetta, a car very similar to the VW Bora in the UK, which I had a lot of experience with. It would take me two to three days to get each of the vehicles fully operational and tested. I stripped the interior of the car completely. Seats, trimming, consoles, carpet and roof lining were removed and laid out on the floor exactly as they had been removed. This would make it easier when putting the car back together. The first job was to run cables from the car's battery to the boot of the car, where it would provide a trickle feed to two main batteries that would supply power to all the control equipment for the surveillance cameras. The trick, as with all the cables and equipment I would be fitting, was to make them blend in and seem part of the original vehicle systems. Only a very close inspection should reveal that they were in fact linked to covert surveillance equipment, and even then only by an experienced surveillance expert. With two large twelve-volt batteries fitted into the boot where the spare wheel had been, the equipment would last for up to two days without having to be recharged. That would leave enough time for one of the other vehicles I was fitting to be put in place to take over the surveillance on the target house. With all the cables now installed, it was time to build the cameras for the vehicles.

There are plenty of so-called covert surveillance cameras available from online spy and gadget shops, but they simply are not good enough for a professional surveillance operation. So I constructed my own purpose-built cameras for each of the vehicles I was fitting out. For the VW Jetta, I decided on two cameras: one fixed and one with full pan, tilt and zoom (PTZ) functions. The fixed camera was fitted to a child's teddy bear, which was Velcroed to the rear parcel shelf. This would give a wide-angle view of anyone approaching the target house from behind the vehicle once it was parked on the street. Building the PTZ camera was far more challenging. Hiding a camera into the headrest of the driver's seat would give

Tommy, back at the control room, the best options for viewing not only the target house, but everyone coming and going from there as well. The problem was it was a very tight fit, and it would have to be identical to the passenger headrest. Painstakingly slow, I fitted the camera and controls to the headrest before covering the lens with a pair of stretched ladies' tights to prevent any sun or car lights reflecting off the lens and giving away the camera's location.

With the cameras now fitted, it was time to put the car back together and test it. It was always the same – despite the countless vehicles I had stripped out and put back together over the years, I always had spare pieces left over. I could see the somewhat worried look on the faces of the three intelligence officers in the garage with me, but I simply smiled and said, 'Perfectly normal. None of these bits are important anyway.' I don't think they were convinced. I had set up a transmit/receive microwave link within the compound to allow us to fully test not only the video signal but the ability to switch between the two cameras in the vehicle and control the PTZ functions. The microwave antenna was hidden in a small cushion positioned on the front passenger seat of the car. After a little tweaking it worked pretty well, but I still had concerns about its functionality once put in place at the target.

In the Merc, I decided to fit one camera into the rear-view mirror and another into the sun visor. Both would give excellent wide-angle views of the street and the entrance to the target house. The bakkie was fitted with another headrest camera and a camera inside a small toolbox left on the dashboard. Finally, all three vehicles were fitted with a stills camera, firing from a small aperture in the boot of the VW and Merc, and from behind the front grill of the bakkie. All the cameras, including the stills camera, could be controlled by the driver of the vehicle using various switches fitted to the console surrounding him, which, of course, looked just like another part of the vehicle controls. The intelligence officers could now drive the vehicle into place, position and focus the cameras where they wanted and leave the vehicle completely unattended but fully visible and controllable from the operations room.

I spent a day going over the operation of the vehicles with Tommy and his two colleagues. They were sharp and asked all the right questions. I went through basic fault-finding with them. Most importantly of all, I showed them on the map exactly where they would have to position the overwatch camera and the microwave link to get the images back to the control room. I had chosen a nearby highway flyover; it was close enough to give good transmission but far enough away not to draw any attention from the target's security detail. It had taken ten days in total and I was exhausted at the end of it. Exhausted and exhilarated all at once – it felt good to be doing something challenging again.

The cars were removed from the compound on the back of flatbed trucks and covered with dust sheets to prevent them being identified on the journey to the operation in Johannesburg. I still knew nothing about the operation or the target, but I was too tired to care, to be honest. Tommy handed me an envelope and offered me one final handshake. I had forgotten about payment so had no idea how much I was getting.

'Wish it was more, but thanks for everything. If I can ever return the favour, just get in touch through Villi,' Tommy said, before exiting the industrial unit. I never saw him again.

My ten days' work earned me R10,000 – about a month's salary for me. It was my first paid covert surveillance job outside of military service, and I suddenly realised how lucrative it could be. Then came the news report of the raid on Zuma's Johannesburg home. In truth, I had never heard of Jacob Zuma. I had little or no interest in South African politics.

That morning Zuma was briefly seen walking outside the house named 'Idle Winds' at 8 Epping Road, Forest Town. Members of the Scorpions were patrolling the house. The Scorpions, officially known as the Directorate of Special Operations (DSO) was an independent multidisciplinary agency that investigated and prosecuted organised crime and corruption. It was a unit of the National Prosecuting Authority of South Africa. Earlier, four men armed with automatic weapons screeched up to the house in a black Jeep with flashing blue lights and ran up to the gate. The men cocked their rifles and told members of the Scorpions to put down their guns. They then entered the premises and were later seen arguing with the Scorpions. Also parked outside the house was a police car marked 'Presidential Protection Unit'. So this was the professional security that Tommy had referred to when briefing me on the job. It made perfect sense why they had kept the operation so secret: it could easily have been leaked to Zuma's security detail or, more lucratively, to the media. Jacob Zuma had been the target all along.

Zuma was charged with two counts of corruption after Shaik was sentenced to fifteen years in jail for fraud and corruption. Despite the charges and the subsequent investigation, Jacob Zuma would go on to become leader of the African National Congress in 2007 and was sworn in as president of South Africa in May 2009 – all this despite the scandals surrounding him. In 2008, the charges against Zuma were dismissed, only to be reinstated in March 2018, mere weeks after Zuma was forced to resign as president. I found it incredible that corruption could occur at such high levels in government. Little did I know what I would discover on returning to Ireland during the era of the Celtic Tiger.

Chapter 3

The Tiger's Roar

It was money for old rope, really. The devices were clearly shop-bought. Although they were amateur, they were still capable of recording conversations, just not remotely. Each had been hidden in different types of everyday objects: a computer mouse, a calculator and a telephone. I had found all three on the first physical search sweep. There was no need for any of the sophisticated search equipment I had with me. I would sweep the room with it anyway, belt and braces, just as I had always been taught. The worrying part for the client, ANZ bank in this case, was that the devices must have been planted by one of their employees. Once the recordings were made, they would have to be retrieved by the culprits at a later stage, but not too long after, otherwise the information recorded would be of little use. It was now down to the client to decide how to proceed. They could remove the devices and improve the security around their offices to prevent further breaches. They could leave the devices as they were and place their own covert surveillance cameras to try and catch the culprit as they retrieved the devices. Or, my favourite tactic, they could leave the devices in place, feed their rivals false information and then apprehend the culprit when enough damage had been inflicted. They took the third option. This meant additional work for me, but I was being well paid, so I wasn't about to complain. The commercial espionage business in Australia was paying off handsomely.

South Africa had just become too dangerous. Despite all the security systems, weapons and precautions that we could take, it still felt unsafe. Fortunately for us we had the option that most South Africans didn't have – immigration. Both of us were UK and Irish passport holders and had qualifications and funds that would allow us to be accepted into most countries. We chose Australia, but we departed South Africa with heavy hearts as we left good friends and family behind. They all understood our difficult decision, and I think many were envious of our ability to up sticks and leave. South Africa was entering a very uncertain stage in its political development, especially for the ageing white minority. Many remembered what had happened in Zimbabwe and were fearful of a similar outcome.

So, here we were, living in the heart of Sydney, in a penthouse apartment overlooking the beautiful Darling Harbour on one side and Sydney Harbour Bridge on the other. I had secured a position as a project manager for TAC, a global supplier of integrated security and building control systems. We were living the good life, at least on the outside, but I was struggling with nightmares and insomnia – a legacy of my life in the military. I was using alcohol and work as a way of dealing with the problem, or as a way of not dealing with it. On arrival in Australia, I made the decision that as soon as we were settled in, I would invest in a full military-grade TSCM kit. This would allow me to work for myself. The contacts I was making with large blue-chip companies through my work with TAC were paying off handsomely. It wasn't long before I had invested over $30,000 in TSCM equipment. I bought only the best from a company called Winkelmann, suppliers to military intelligence units worldwide. It had paid for itself within six months. My daily charge was $1,000 plus expenses. No one ever even questioned my fees and I rarely appeared on anyone's books. No one wanted to admit to utilising this type of service.

Within a year I hated Sydney. It was just like any other city, just hotter. I was working every hour possible, not because I had to but because I wanted to. Steff and I rarely saw each other, and we really weren't making the most of the Australian lifestyle. We made the decision to move to Queensland, just outside of Brisbane, to see if the slower pace of life would make things better. It didn't. I worked just as hard, switching between project management and counter-surveillance jobs. I was now well experienced in commercial espionage and counter-espionage, and was the go-to man for many large financial institutions in Queensland.

Despite the professional and therefore financial success I was experiencing, I still had one eye on what was happening at home. The boom had well and truly landed in Ireland. It was even making headlines in Australia. Ex-council houses in Dublin were selling for €500,000. All my friends in Australia thought it was madness, and it turns out they were right. While long-term renting in Australia and other parts of the world is perfectly normal, there is something in the Irish psyche about owning your own home. It's ingrained in us. Things weren't going too well between Steff and I anyway, so I sat down one evening with her and convinced her that heading home to Ireland would be the best thing for us. She was completely against it initially. She loved Australia; it was everything South Africa should have been for us. In the end she gave in, but really we were only delaying the inevitable split in our relationship. I would head back first and get set up with a job and a place to live, with Steff following on later. Everyone we knew in Australia advised against our move back, and everyone in Ireland thought it was a great idea. Within weeks I was on a flight bound for Dublin, running away from the nightmares again, hoping that another fresh start would finally put them to rest.

Ireland had changed a lot in the years I had been away. The place was awash with money. Brand-new cars, designer clothes and mansion-style houses were everywhere. I decided to rent an apartment in Malahide, just outside Dublin, as that was where I was most likely to get work. I had my first job secured within a week, working as a security consultant, on a sub-contract basis, on a number of large projects around Dublin, including the National Conference Centre (NCC). While security design projects were interesting, it wasn't where my real plans lay. With the contacts I was making with developers on the design side, I decided to start testing the water to see if there was any appetite for commercial counter-espionage work. At first no one seemed to know what I was talking about, but when I clarified it as 'bug-sweeping', I got my first few bites.

My first few counter-surveillance operations were basic TSCM sweeps. They were routine safeguards carried out by large companies and financial institutions about every six months or so. This is good practice, and when accompanied by additional sweeps when large deals are in the offing, it usually ensures that the boardrooms and offices of senior figures are not subject to any illicit eavesdropping. Among my very first clients in Ireland was Pfizer, the international pharmaceutical giant. Their commercial offices were located in Citywest Business Campus just outside Dublin. Two things struck me about them. Firstly, for such a large company, the physical security of their premises was appalling. Secondly, their knowledge of what Information Security (InfoSec) really meant and how to counter any attempt to compromise it was truly shocking. I was met by a security consultant and given the access keys and cards required to enter the building. I wouldn't have needed them. I could have walked in with the cleaners, as I learned later that evening. Despite his position as Security Consultant, he was upfront about the gaps in his knowledge and was keen to learn more. I recommended a number of courses for him to attend. I'm not sure if he ever did, though. The sweep was routine in every way and I was slightly concerned that the TSCM business in Ireland would be very hit and miss. If this was the benchmark then it wouldn't be a viable business for me to pursue. I couldn't have been more wrong!

It was a couple of weeks before I got my second TSCM job, following a random call from a security manager of a pharmaceutical company named Alza/Cordis, a Johnson & Johnson subsidiary located on the Cahir Road in Cashel. The CEO was worried about possible leaks and/or bugging of the offices and meeting rooms located within the building. It was blatantly obvious that this was the first time they had used the services of a TSCM operator. The security manager wanted assurances that no one would know what I was actually up to and that any invoices were to reflect this. I explained fully that my services would be totally discreet and billing could be in any format that he wished, including cash. I made the long journey to Cashel on a Saturday morning, when the plant would be at its quietest. I gave a name and company (neither of them real) at the front desk and received my ID and pass card. I carried out the sweep over two days, but within minutes of being on-site, I knew what the problem was, and it wasn't that the offices were bugged. The walls of the offices were paper-thin and every word being uttered could be heard outside. At the debrief with the security manager, he was more than a little red-faced when I pointed this out to him. A simple process of insulating the walls and maintaining a routine TSCM schedule would eradicate any potential loss of intellectual property.

By this stage, Steff had arrived from Australia and secured herself a job as a PA to the CEO of a large company based in Dublin. She seemed happy with the way things were, although our relationship was still very strained. Within days of the Cashel job, I had my next enquiry, this time from a high-net-worth individual, a former CEO now turned consultant. It was to be the beginning of an avalanche of work that utterly shocked me. Ireland was as much a part of the world of commercial espionage as anywhere else I had been, perhaps even more so. It seemed some of those at the top of Irish industry had a lot more to hide and were willing to spend a lot of money to ensure it remained hidden.

Chapter 4

Tricks and Tools of the Trade

Wars are won and lost based on which side has the best intelligence, and the business world is no different. Keeping information secure is of vital importance. The battle between those trying to steal information and those trying to keep information secure is never-ending. The murky world of Irish business, which ultimately led to the country's downfall, was ever active in this battle for information. To fully understand the operations that I was involved in, it is first necessary to understand how commercial espionage is carried out and the devastating effects it can have.

Corporate espionage accounts for losses totalling €600 million in Ireland and €400 billion globally every year. While it is estimated that a large portion of this is lost through cyberespionage, the use of illicit and illegal covert audio and video surveillance devices is on the increase. Huge investments by governments and large corporations into cybersecurity have resulted in computer hacking becoming more and more difficult. As a result, would-be commercial spies are turning their attention to good old-fashioned human intelligence or 'Humint' as it is known in military circles. Humint deals with the physical loss of information outside of the IT network via human sources – using real people and traditional spycraft. Such a loss of information can have grave consequences such as reputational damage, a drop in share price due to insider trading and the loss of a competitive edge regarding rival companies and business partners. Company employees and sub-contractors often pose the greatest threat, as they already have physical access to a company premises. The fact that they are already employees makes them very difficult to apprehend.

Devices are now much smaller and far more advanced than ever before. Easy to plant and to retrieve, they are a real threat to any organisation's InfoSec. As well as high street gadget shops, devices can be sourced online on sites such as www.spyequipmentuk.co.uk and www.eyetek.co.uk. No licence is required to purchase them and no register is kept of who is buying them. The following are some of the devices freely available on the open market for anyone to purchase and use.

GSM Bug Long-Life Audio-Listening Device

This voice-activated GSM bug gives you the ability to dial into the unit and listen to surrounding sounds with startling clarity. The bug can be programmed by SMS commands to dial any number you choose when it detects sound or speech. This ensures that the 'spy' does not miss any of the conversations that might be taking place. The intelligent GSM bug operates on the GSM frequency 1800 and 1900MHz communications network for worldwide coverage. The sound-activation function can be switched on and off by SMS commands, and the spy can dial into it at any time. This unit contains a 5,200 mAh Li-Ion battery, giving it up to six weeks' battery life in standby mode. This bug is capable of being secreted into any position and is very difficult to detect. (Size: 70 x 40 x 40 mm. Cost: €95)

USB Data Stick 25-Day Covert Voice Recorder

With up to twenty-five days in standby mode and twenty-four hours of continuous recording, this is a very popular device among those in the illicit eavesdropping trade. When a long battery life and long recording time are required, this voice-activated miniature recorder ticks all of the boxes for any would-be spy. When the surrounding area is silent, recording is paused, and as soon as sound is detected, it will start recording again. This enables the memory and battery to be used with maximum efficiency. Each recording is time- and date-stamped, giving a valuable record when used for evidential purposes. This device is often used in the bugging of offices and vehicles. Considering the amount of USB sticks lying around homes and offices, this device raises no suspicion. (Cost: €120)

Air Freshener Hidden Voice-Activated Recorder Device

This air freshener contains a concealed security, high-quality, voice-activated voice recorder that boasts up to 100 days in standby and 185 hours of recording on a fully charged battery. The recorder has the capability of recording for up to eight weeks based on three hours of recording per day. This device has a time and date stamp on the recording. Again, this device is perfect for offices and homes, as it is unlikely to raise any suspicion. (Cost: €180)

Tissue Box Camera Recorder

This camera, hidden in a tissue box, is undetectable and inconspicuous. It has a built-in battery that can power it for up to sixteen hours and up to a 32GB capacity (sixty-four hours of actual recording time). It's one of the best on the market, as no one would even give it a second glance. (Cost: €320)

GSM Bug USB Charger Audio-Listening Device

This USB type charger can be found in many homes and business premises. The difference with this one is it contains a highly sensitive microphone connected to a GSM transmitter with its own SIM card, thus enabling you to dial into it from anywhere in the world. Once plugged into the mains, this USB charger is powered up and ready to dial into. Simply dial the SIM card number inside the USB power supply and wherever you are in the world it will automatically and silently connect, transmitting any conversations and sounds over the GSM network from up to thirty feet away from the charger. Sound is filtered for perfect audio clarity. The USB charger camera is quad band and operates with worldwide coverage. To the naked eye this looks like nothing more than a casual USB charger, but it secretly allows anyone to monitor everything in that room without sound distortion. Note that this is a fully functional USB power supply and will charge any device plugged into it. (Cost: €220)

These are just a small sample of the devices available for public purchase, but they are amateur in comparison to what is available to law enforcement and intelligence agencies around the world. From my own experience with intelligence agencies, their capabilities are truly shocking. So how can companies mitigate against such eavesdropping devices? Internal audit programs carried out by businesses cannot detect all threats. Electronic eavesdropping threats are rarely even mentioned in most reports and this includes the threat of potential loss of information over cellular networks. Preventative TSCM is essential to prevent the loss of valuable corporate information and should be incorporated into any InfoSec framework. Preventing the success of corporate espionage attempts is challenging.

So what is TSCM?

TSCM stands for Technical Surveillance Countermeasures. In layman's terms, it is the method and equipment used to detect, locate and neutralise any illicit covert audio or video surveillance device. Any information not protected by an organisation's cybersecurity system – that lies outside of the IT network – can be exploited. Everything from audio and video recorders to keyloggers can be used to steal valuable information. A routine TSCM sweep should start with a physical search of the target area and be followed by an electronic sweep. Searching for phone-taps, wiretaps and wireless devices is another essential part of the TSCM search procedure. A fingertip physical search was at the forefront of my approach and should be for any TSCM firm, but I also had state-of-the-art counter-surveillance equipment to back me up. At the time of writing, my equipment consists of the following.

Non-Linear Junction Detector (NLJD)

My handheld ORION HX Deluxe Non-Linear Junction Detector (NLJD) has interchangeable 2.4 GHz and 900 MHz antenna heads and is used to sweep areas for electronic semi-conductor components. I use it to locate hidden electronics or eavesdropping devices regardless of whether the electronic device is turned on. It can detect both small, modern circuitry in office environments with the 2.4 antenna and older, less refined circuitry through dense materials with the 900 antenna. It's a costly piece of equipment at €10,000, but it's worth it.

OSCOR Green Spectrum Analyser

This highly portable RF Detection & Spectrum Analyser is designed to detect illicit eavesdropping signals, perform site surveys for communication systems, conduct radio frequency (RF) emissions analysis and investigate misuse of the RF spectrum. The OSCOR Green is a portable spectrum analyser that sweeps 24 GHz in one second to quickly detect transmitting electronic surveillance devices and ensure that spectrum activity is captured. This piece of equipment will set you back a cool €22,000.

A communications jammer and in-place monitoring system for use with GSM, 3G and 4G signals also forms part of my kit. Thermal cameras, UV pens, inspection lights, telephone analysers and a handheld signal are all essential parts of my TSCM toolkit. Some might think that the cost of a TSCM sweep is excessive, but as you can see from the cost of the equipment, it is perfectly justifiable. It is also essential to keep abreast of new advances in TSCM and in the very covert surveillance equipment you are trying to detect.

On my return to Ireland, I found numerous firms advertising themselves as TSCM professionals – advertising was something I never did – and yet they had not invested in the correct equipment to do the job properly. Many private investigators fall within this category; some have no police or military background whatsoever, which calls into question where they were trained in TSCM. All the knowledge I had gained in both the military and commercial world of espionage would help me to build a large client base in Ireland. It was the scale and diversity of companies and individuals that were looking for my services in Ireland that was greatly surprising. Ireland, as I was quickly going to learn, had a very dark underbelly hiding beneath its global success.

Chapter 5

Anglo Irish Bank – 'The Best Bank in the World'

It was almost midnight and I had been sitting in a parked van on St Stephen's Green, Dublin, for over three hours. I had hired the van a few days earlier, kitted it out with roof ladders and thrown some tools in the back. I never used my own personal vehicles on jobs like this. It was disguised as just another building-services vehicle, one of the tens of thousands roaming around the country, thanks to the development book of the Celtic Tiger. The only break I had taken was a walk around the Green, not to stretch my legs but to scan for the tell-tale signs of somebody watching either me or the building I was about to enter.

There was no indication of any suspect vehicle, nor were there any eyes lingering on me for longer than they should have. Taxi drivers and the last of the late-night revellers were all that remained on the streets that night. I had paid a few random visits to the Green over the previous three days, trying to spot any surveillance on the building, but there had been no obvious sign of a mobile-listening post within an operational distance of the building. Of course, there may have been a static post set up in one of the adjacent buildings, hence my visit tonight. I sat across the street at an angle from the entrance to the building, using my mirrors to keep an eye on the doorway and the approaches to it. Satisfied that I was alone, I got out of the van and started to unload the necessary kit. A toolbox, a stepladder and two flight cases contained everything I would require, but it was a struggle to get them to the door in one trip. I had no intentions of making a second trip – the less that was seen of me, the better.

It was a bitterly cold night, which was the perfect excuse to be wearing a hooded jacket and gloves, but the weather wasn't the reason I had those on. The hood would prevent any CCTV surveillance cameras from identifying me as I entered the building, and the gloves hid the pair of latex gloves I was wearing beneath them, ensuring I would leave no fingerprints behind. I got to the entrance, carefully keeping my head down, and then used the key and the pass card that had been supplied to me to enter the building. It was a dark winter night in early 2007, and I had just entered the headquarters of Anglo Irish Bank. Time to get to work!

To be clear, my entrance into Anglo Irish Bank headquarters in Dublin was by invitation. I was not a burglar or doing anything illegal, but in this line of work discretion is a must. The gloves were essential; after all, I wasn't sure if I was the first TSCM operator to be used by this company and I had no idea if anything illicit had been left behind by any predecessors. I was not taking the chance of having any suspicions pointing in my direction. It was not uncommon for companies conducting sweeps on behalf of one company to plant devices on behalf of a rival company – a dangerous game to play but a very lucrative one.

I entered the building and approached the security guard on duty to identify myself. He was expecting the name I gave him, although it wasn't mine. Then I headed straight for the CCTV control system. I immediately set about disabling the CCTV surveillance cameras. I didn't want anyone looking back at the footage later to see what I had been up to. The security guard was under the impression that I was there to work on the system and so took no further notice of me. With the CCTV system now offline, it was time to get down to the work I was really there to do. There were several rooms on my list that night: those of the Chief Executive Officer (CEO) and the Chief Financial Officer (CFO), the server room and several meeting rooms. Not all the rooms on the list were in the main building but in the adjacent townhouses that formed part of the company's headquarters.

I decided to start at the top and work my way down the chain of command. First on the list was the CEO, and I immediately recognised the name on the doorplate. David Drumm was heralded as the man behind one of Ireland's greatest financial success stories – a remarkable achievement for a man from relatively humble beginnings. Drumm was born in Skerries, a seaside town in north Co. Dublin, and was educated by the Christian Brothers before joining Deloitte & Touche to train as a chartered accountant. His career in finance began in 1988 when he took a position with the International Fund for Ireland, helping to finance new business start-ups. Drumm then moved to Anglo Irish Bank as an assistant manager and, by 1995, he had been promoted to a manager's position.

Anglo Irish Bank was different to other banks in that it lent to smaller clients, in particular those that may have been refused by the larger lending institutions. Although it was a risky strategy, it was proving to be quite lucrative for now at least. In 1997, Drumm, along with his family – his wife Lorraine and two daughters – moved to Boston to set up Anglo's business operations there. James Pappas, a friend of CEO Seán FitzPatrick, was Drumm's first major deal there: a $20 million loan to build the Harbor Point Market Place in Dorchester. From there Drumm went on to much bigger deals, offering large sums over longer periods to entice developers in and to trump his competitors. He soon earned the nickname of 'Drummer' and a reputation for extensive business tactics, including taking developers on expensive golf outings in the USA and Ireland. Anglo's tactic of targeting developers was paying off handsomely; deals were struck with National Development, one of Boston's largest commercial builders, and Anglo's loan book expanded to almost $300 million.

By the time he was thirty-five, Drumm had made the meteoric rise through the Anglo ranks to the position of head of Irish lending. It was a just reward for growing their US business from nothing to $4.3 billion in gross assets. But it was in 2005 that the shock decision came from Seán FitzPatrick to have David Drumm succeed him as CEO of Anglo. The three clear front runners – Tiarnan O'Mahony, the chief operating officer, Tom Brown, head of wealth management and John Rowan, head of Anglo UK – were all passed over.

Drumm's business model for Anglo now intensified. The pursuit of developers increased, even to the level of finding and identifying projects for developers to pursue so that Anglo could lend them the money to build. Drumm was known as a plain speaker, and this endeared him to many of the developers who found him different and easier to deal with than other lenders in the market.

Profits rose by 70% in Drumm's first three years in charge and Anglo seemed to be living a charmed life. Everything they touched seemed to turn to gold.

I entered Drumm's office, careful to keep the lights switched off until I had closed the blinds. I stripped off my hooded jacket and outer gloves but kept the latex gloves on. I set the flight cases down in the corner of the room. Each contained incredibly expensive and highly sophisticated equipment, but I wouldn't be needing them yet. Just like the overt CCTV cameras inside and outside the building, I wanted to find any potential covert CCTV cameras hidden in the room. I took the covert CCTV detector from the toolbox. Its powerful infrared beam would be reflected by any hidden video camera's optics and would be easily detected by me. The IR-filtering glass built into the detector avoids natural reflections from surfaces and concentrates on finding the exact location of hidden cameras. Once the room was scanned, I took out the digital camera from my toolbox and began photographing everything in the room. The location of pens, folders, furniture, etc. was recorded. Everything would be returned to its original position before I left, and the digital images would ensure that it was exactly right.

I always started a job with a fingertip search of the room. While the electronic search equipment I had was state-of-the-art, I had been taught by my British Intelligence instructors that a physical search was always the best way to locate a covert device. Items that I knew often contained such devices were checked first: pens, power extension leads, computer mouse and smoke and fire alarms. A device could be fitted to almost anything. I searched the telephone handset for any bug that might have been implanted in it. Later, I would check the telephone exchange for any hardwired taps to the phone lines. The windows were inspected for any bugs that may have been attached by adhesive material to either the interior or exterior – a common enough tactic.

I checked the computer for a keylogger, sometimes called a keystroke logger or system monitor, which is a hardware device that monitors each keystroke a user types on a specific computer's keyboard. Next, I thoroughly searched the furniture, turning it upside down and physically searching for anything that might have been hidden. I carefully removed the pictures from the walls, some of which were probably quite valuable, and looked for any device concealed in the frames. The hardest part of the physical search was removing the cover plates of every power socket and datapoint in the room; it was tedious and time-consuming. Satisfied they hadn't been interfered with, I reassembled them and placed a tamper-proof seal on them. Invisible to the naked eye, the seals could later be checked with a UV light to ensure that the cover plate had not been tampered with. Next, I extended the folding ladder and inspected the walls and ceiling for anything that might have been secreted into them. With the physical search complete, it was now time to bring the electronic equipment online.

The Non-Linear Junction Detector (NLJD), designed for the detection of both active and passive electronic components and devices, can detect all types of eavesdropping equipment, such as receiver-transmitter or radio-electronic devices, including mobile phone SIM cards, voice recorders, radio bugs or any listening device. I kept it in the flight case to protect it from prying eyes and to ensure such a valuable piece of equipment never got damaged. Like the fingertip search, everything in the room was swept but with much greater speed and efficiency. Any electronic device hidden within the room would be picked up by the handheld detector.

Finally, it was time to bring out the most expensive and technically advanced piece of equipment: the RF detection scanner. Capable of intercepting analogue and digital radio signals, along with GSM and Wi-Fi, this was top-of-the-line equipment. I placed an iPod in the room along with several transmitter/receivers then left with the base station. I put my headphones on and set the control equipment to scan. If there was a listening device in the room, the equipment would pick up the signal and I would hear the music from the iPod in my headset. The full scan could run up to thirty minutes, but when it was complete I would know for certain whether or not there was eavesdropping equipment or covert CCTV cameras in the room.

I packed up my kit and moved on to the next office. The name on the door was alien to me, not as high-profile as either Drumm or FitzPatrick. Willie McAteer was from Donegal and a graduate of UCD with a BA in Commerce and an MA in Business Studies. He too went on to become a qualified chartered accountant and a member of the Irish Tax Institute. McAteer became a partner at PwC and a managing director of the venture capital lending company, Yeoman International Leasing. In 1992, he joined Anglo as finance director and was there for fifteen years, also serving on the Board of Executive Directors. Drumm relied heavily on him during his first years as CEO of Anglo, and Drumm gave him the added responsibility for risk as well as finance.

I carried out the same procedure in each room. Some of those meeting rooms would have been used by the chairman of the Anglo board, the now-infamous Seán

FitzPatrick, the son of a small farmer. His mother was a civil servant, but she left her position to raise her children, Seán and his older sister, Joyce. Joyce would later go on to become the sixth President of the National College of Ireland, while Seán continued his education at University College Dublin. He was CEO of Anglo Irish Bank from 1986 to 2005, when he moved into the position of chairman. For his last full year in control, profit before tax stood at €504 million, lending had reached €24 billion and lending for 2004 alone came in at €6.3 billion, up 35% on the previous year – truly spectacular results. Over a decade, the bank went from gross assets of just £3.14 billion (€4 billion) in 1997 to €95 billion by the end of 2007. In 1997, it was worth just €250 million. In 2007, it was worth €12.4 billion, ranking fourth on the stock exchange league table after AIB, CRH and Bank of Ireland. In 1997, you could have bought Anglo shares for just 81p (€1.03). In February 2007, they had climbed to €16.10. Anyone who bought 1,000 Anglo shares for €1,030 in 1997 would have shares worth €32,220 a decade later – an unbelievable return. But something was very wrong at Anglo Irish Bank and these three men would later be at the heart of it. The trouble was that I didn't know just what it was, yet.

As a TSCM specialist, and more importantly as a British military-trained counter-surveillance expert, now with considerable experience in commercial espionage, I suspected something wasn't right. The first thing you learn in the world of commercial espionage is that the client rarely tells you the whole story. In fact, they often outright lie to you. Sometimes it's to protect sensitive information but, more often than not, it's because they themselves are involved in something illicit. Everything about these Anglo sweeps was wrong. TSCM sweeps are not cheap, my services certainly weren't. Anglo didn't seem to care. Even though I had fitted the covert seals on the sockets and datapoints – which was meant to speed up the process of TSCM, and therefore reduce the cost – Anglo were insisting that a full sweep be carried out each time. It was highly unusual. Also, the number of sweeps I was carrying out was hugely excessive: every four to six weeks. On several occasions, I pointed out that I was certain the company was not under any electronic surveillance and that they were in fact wasting their money. But my advice was not taken. Companies, even high-profile banks, normally carry out sweeps routinely; twice a year is considered good practice, or maybe when they are in the middle of a big deal. Sometimes, if they are in the midst of some litigation or perhaps the focus of a hostile takeover, they might order additional checks.

As far as I could ascertain, none of the above applied to Anglo and that set alarm bells ringing. Something else was going on here and I was being kept very much in the dark. But Anglo were paying their bills, so I carried on taking the work. I was starting to assemble some of the pieces, but it would be another while before it all came together and I would find myself as one part of a very dark period in Irish history.

Chapter 6

Rugby Sweeps

It was Kev alright, no mistaking the big ugly Scottish head on him. I didn't attempt to approach him though; it was obvious he was on a job. He was wearing an official security pass card around his neck, and I immediately recognised the flight cases he was carrying: TSCM equipment. My old mate from the bad old days in Northern Ireland had scored himself VIP access to the game. Lucky sod! It was November 2005, and England were playing the All Blacks at Twickenham. I was back from South Africa for a few weeks before our move to Australia, and a chance to see the All Blacks playing was too good an opportunity to miss. Steff and I had decided to make a weekend of it in London and catch up with old friends at the same time. There had been rumours leading up to the match about the England team taking precautions against any attempt at skullduggery, but a full sweep on the day of the match was a bit excessive. The game went well, if you were an All Blacks fan, 19-23 to the New Zealanders. I dropped Kev a quick message to see if he was up for a beer after the game. I got a swift reply: 'Usual place?' The usual place for any meet after a rugby match for JCU-NI members, past or present, was the Union Jack Club in London.

It was good to see him. He was always jolly, with a quick sense of humour, but was a devil for the drink. The pints were soon flowing and I couldn't help myself from asking about the job at Twickenham. 'A bit OTT, mate, a full sweep just before the match?'

Kev downed the last of his pint and nodded at the barmaid for another round. 'Not at all, mate. Things have gotten very heavy in the sports world, a lot riding on these games now.' He was smirking and I knew that there was more to come.

I probed a little further. 'A quick sweep job, then perfect seats for the match too, I bet?'

Alcohol and secrets don't mix. It had been the downfall of many a military operation throughout the years.

'What makes you think I was doing a sweep? Didn't see a single minute of that match, mate. I was busy. All Blacks aren't the only ones who can play that game!' He burst into laughter and headed for the toilets.

I was flabbergasted. Had they bugged the All Blacks to gain valuable live information? Although it hadn't made any difference to the final result, it was certainly an eye-opener. I would soon learn that this was not an isolated incident; even our own national team would have problems with leaks.

'The first thing to remember about rugby is that it's a physical fight' is a quote I remember from the *Irish Times* rugby correspondent Gerry Thornley. He was right, but coming a close second was the psychological battle – just as dirty and sometimes more devastating. That was the thought running through my head as I reflected on the job I had just completed for the IRFU.

It was the summer of 2008 in the Ballsbridge Hotel, which is located a short distance down the road from the Irish Rugby Football Union's (IRFU) headquarters on Dublin's Lansdowne Road. It was time for another IRFU committee meeting, but this would be, in many ways, the first of its kind. The IRFU is the governing body for Rugby Union in Ireland. Each affiliated rugby club throughout the country nominates a member to their provincial branch committee, and each branch elects members to the IRFU committee. Those men were now seated before me; for months there had been an air of suspicion hanging over them. I studied each of the men gathered around the large boardroom table carefully and, clearly, there were a few worried faces among them. I wondered which one of them it had been, or had there been a number involved? For the past thirty minutes, a colleague and I had delivered a presentation to the IRFU committee on the dangers of modern information security, covert surveillance devices and press leaks. But it would be the next few minutes that would really rattle them.

'Despite what I have just told you, none of this technology poses the greatest threat to the IRFU's confidential information. These devices can be militated against using Technical Surveillance Countermeasures at our disposal. It is those of you sitting around this table that pose the real threat.'

A few shifted uncomfortably in their seats. They had no idea where this was leading but knew full well where it had all begun.

It had started months before at another IRFU committee meeting in Dublin's plush Shelbourne Hotel on St Stephen's Green. Among the items on the agenda was the fate of Ireland's head coach, Eddie O'Sullivan. A native Cork man, O'Sullivan was, at the time, considered to be one of

Ireland's most successful coaches. However, the 2007 World Cup had been a disaster for Irish rugby, with rumours of problems within the camp even before the tournament had begun. Skirmishes between Munster and Leinster players before the contest were reported to be a serious issue, and the possibility of Brian O'Driscoll leaving to play club rugby in France, or even retiring completely, was well publicised. O'Sullivan's trademark authoritarian grip was slipping, and morale along with creativity and flair were suffering. The claim by O'Driscoll in one interview before the World Cup that Ireland would 'go all the way' only made their dismal performance all the worse.

With three Triple Crowns in four years, O'Sullivan's achievements were not to be belittled, but further recent failures would prove to be too much for the IRFU to endure. O'Sullivan's departure was almost guaranteed once he failed to win his three home matches of the 2008 Six Nations tournament. The Six Nations spanking by England removed any lingering doubts regarding his fate. The IRFU released a statement that really didn't confirm or deny anything. It simply read, 'The IRFU shares in the disappointment with the out-turn of this year's RBS Six Nations Championship from an Irish perspective and will be undertaking a detailed review of our performance. Our objective in this, as always, will be to ensure the Irish rugby team has in place the optimal structures to allow it to perform at the highest international levels into the future.' But behind the scenes, preparations were being made for O'Sullivan's departure.

In the following days, the contents of the IRFU committee meeting at the Shelbourne Hotel made their way into the Irish media, almost word for word. It was the 'almost word for word' part that raised red flags with CEO

Phillip Browne. He was concerned that the meeting had been subject to some form of covert surveillance, either directly by members of the media or by a commercial agency willing to sell the transcripts to the highest bidder – or worse, by one of the committee members themselves. Not only had O'Sullivan's impending departure been reported, so had the fact that negotiations were taking place between the IRFU and O'Sullivan's representatives about a settlement. O'Sullivan had been given a controversial four-year contract before the 2007 World Cup that he would need to be compensated for. Word was there would be an outwardly amicable parting of the ways, although privately that may not have been the case. John Baker, O'Sullivan's shrewd agent, and the Union would agree a package close to €500,000 (about a year and a half's salary) to compensate him for the termination of that contract. All of this was now in the public domain and proving very embarrassing for the IRFU.

The subject of O'Sullivan's successor was also open for discussion at the meeting, although it was by no means finalised. The search for a replacement, not only for the head coach but also for other members of the management team, all of whom were now out of contract, would shortly get under way. There was a lengthy list of possible candidates for O'Sullivan's position. Among the contenders was Jake White, who had seen highs and lows during his tenure as head coach with the South African Springboks. A below-average performance in 2006 was followed by World Cup triumph for the Boks in France in 2007. However, White was rumoured to be in the sights of England rugby, who had a much larger chequebook than the IRFU. Declan Kidney, the man behind the 2006 Munster Heineken Cup victory, was also in the mix. Kidney had served as second in command to Eddie O'Sullivan before a very short and unsuccessful time at Newport Gwent Dragons. After a Heineken Cup quarter-final loss to Leicester during a year in charge at Leinster, Kidney returned to Munster and had tasted success. Wayne Smith, the current 2008 All Blacks assistant coach, had, just like O'Sullivan, been subject to severe criticism for his team's quarter-final exit from the 2007 World Cup. Despite the poor performance, Smith was also reported to be in the IRFU's sights. Pat Howard, another Antipodean, now the Australian Rugby Union's high-performance unit manager, had also been mentioned. A tremendous spell of success with the Leicester Tigers would have given him the perfect pedigree for the Ireland job, but family commitments in Australia may well have ruled him out of the running. Other names reported to be possibilities were Michael Bradley, Niall O'Donovan, John Mitchell and Eddie Jones, although all were considered to be outside chances.

The trouble with these leaks in the media was that it made it very difficult for the IRFU to negotiate in private with any of these individuals. Many of these men would not want their current employers to know that they were even talking to the IRFU. It seemed to Phillip Browne that the media knew every move the IRFU was making. This was a very worrying development, and Browne's concerns were fully justified.

This wasn't the first time that sport had been the subject of covert surveillance scandals – far from it. The sporting world was now a multibillion-dollar global industry. Rugby Union alone generates more than £150 million in revenue and the 2007–2008 season would see Irish rugby players entering a new era of the highly paid professional. While not at the same level of salaries as their soccer counterparts, professional rugby players were beginning to reap the rewards of the increase in popularity of their sport. But just like soccer, rugby players were starting to come under media scrutiny. Their private lives would no longer be that – private! They were now fair game. Ronan O'Gara was one of the first to experience this when it was wrongly reported in the French media during the 2007 Rugby World Cup that his marriage was in trouble due to gambling debts he had accrued. O'Gara rose above the reports, but it was now plain to see that the media honeymoon for IRFU players was over. I suppose a fair question to ask is this: is covert surveillance a real threat in sport? The simple answer is a resounding yes.

In 2003, Clive Woodward, the England rugby coach, admitted that his team's hotel rooms and changing-room facilities had been swept for bugs. Woodward made the admission after hinting that the British and Irish Lions may have been the victims of Australian spying in the 2001 series Down Under. He stopped short of accusing the Australians of planting bugs in the run-up to the final, but said that England was taking precautions just in case. In 2017, the British and Irish Lions routinely swept their facilities at the team's hotels for listening devices to prevent team secrets getting out before the test series against the All Blacks.

Nelson Mandela's former bodyguard says the All Blacks team were poisoned in 1995. As a former top South African police commander involved with All Blacks security at the 1995 Rugby World Cup, he says the team was deliberately poisoned before the final against the Springboks. Rory Steyn – chief bodyguard to President Nelson Mandela – believes betting syndicates were behind the poisoning. The All Blacks lost the Johannesburg final

15-12. Mr Steyn said there was a huge degree of paranoia within the All Blacks camp, which escalated after the semi-final win over England in Cape Town. The team travelled back to Johannesburg and it was decided among management that they would eat separately to the rest of the hotel's guests in the week leading up to the final. 'I said that makes it easier to target them. I didn't think it was a good idea,' Mr Steyn said. It is believed that the team's water was the source of the poisoning.

In 2005, Manchester United Football Club was subject to a covert surveillance operation prior to a vital game against arch-rivals Chelsea. The team's dressing room had been bugged by an unknown individual. That person had managed to smuggle a transmitter past the club's security guards, stewards and even police who were on duty. The resulting two hours of recordings, contained on two tapes, were then put up for sale. The recordings were expected to fetch thousands of pounds, a handsome return for the would-be spook. The content of the tapes was media gold. Sir Alex Ferguson's pre-match pep talk could be heard, as he told his players to go out and enjoy the game. Perhaps not what you would have expected from the often-fiery Scot. Half-time recordings have Sir Alex telling his players to keep the ball away from Chelsea centre-half John Terry and to put tighter marking on Chelsea playmaker Claude Makélélé in midfield. At the end of the game, the team can be heard celebrating, having beaten Chelsea 1-0. While the tapes were only offered for sale after the match, they would have been far more valuable had they been provided live to Chelsea during the match. That's what I would have done, had I been on the covert surveillance side of that operation. A middleman, acting on behalf of the culprit, told the media that plans were already in place to bug further matches. Despite assurances by Manchester United that they would track down the person who planted the device, no one was ever apprehended.

In March 2010, another bug was found and again it involved English football at the heart of that operation. This time the England international team, who were based at a Hertfordshire hotel, found themselves at the wrong end of a surveillance operation prior to their upcoming friendly match against Egypt. The illegal device was found in a hotel meeting room that the team were using. Up to six hours of recordings were covertly obtained, including where England players are heard discussing bonuses they wanted for succeeding at the World Cup in South Africa. Speculation that player sex scandals were joked about on tape added further embarrassment to the breach of security. Most damaging of all was the fact that the team manager, Fabio Capello, had discussed tactics during the meeting. Preparation for any major tournament involves discretion and secrecy. Even the slightest piece of information can give the opposition the upper hand, and in a game that now involves billions of dollars, that advantage can prove to be hugely lucrative. Once again, the culprit was unknown and although an investigation was launched by the English FA, it was to no avail.

Rugby Union is by no means a stranger to bugging scandals. As recently as 2016, the famous New Zealand All Blacks were reported to have been the victims of a 'spying' operation. Days before the opening match of the 2016 Bledisloe Cup, between the All Blacks and the Australian Wallabies, a device was reportedly found in a team meeting room at the InterContinental hotel in Sydney. There were several curious aspects to the discovery of this device, apart from the fact that it had been planted in the first place.

Firstly, the type of bug found was initially reported to have been of the quality used by 'law enforcement and spying agencies'. That can mean only one of two things: either a government-backed agency was responsible, which was highly unlikely, or someone with that type of background was involved. Those of us who are military-trained in the areas of surveillance and counter-surveillance were taught to build our own surveillance devices. And so, when we leave the service and enter private employment, we tend to continue with our own creations. It was then reported that it was an 'off-the-shelf commercial bug', hence anyone could have been responsible.

Secondly, the device was found in the foam of a chair during a routine sweep on the Monday but was not reported to the police until the Saturday, the day of the game. The reason given by the All Blacks management was that they were waiting for NZRU chief Steve Tew to arrive in Sydney from the Rio Olympics before taking the matter further. Most bizarre of all was the man who was charged with public mischief over the bugging affair: 51-year-old Adrian Gard was understood to be a consultant for BGI Security, which was contracted by the All Blacks during their Bledisloe Cup campaign. BGI Security's website advertised its relationship with the All Blacks and a variety of celebrities including Oprah Winfrey, Hugh Jackman, Mick Jagger, the Olsen twins and many more. Gard was listed as an operations employee with a quote: 'We build mutually beneficial partnerships with our clients, continually seeking the best for them and ourselves through innovation and excellence.' So why would Gard plant a device against his own client? There are several possibilities, chief among them being personal gain. He may well have accepted an additional contract to bug the room for another client, completely unbeknown to his employer. Another possibility was an effort to make himself, or his company, look good by supposedly 'finding' a covert device. Unfortunately, many in the TSCM industry stay in business by spreading fear of potential risk, so the occasional 'find' doesn't do their business any harm. Whatever the reason, BGI Consultants refused to comment on the matter. Later, after appearing in court, Adrian Gard was found not guilty of all charges.

Meanwhile, back in Dublin, the IRFU decided it was time to call in the experts, and so they did, or at least they thought they did! My first involvement with the IRFU was as an observer. I was asked to attend an IRFU team meeting at the Ballsbridge Hotel. I was met at the IRFU HQ, just a few hundred metres away, by CEO Phillip Browne. There I was fully briefed on the situation about the recent press leaks. The IRFU, through Browne, had taken steps to militate against further leaks by bringing in a TSCM firm to sweep any further meetings of the team or the committee. My job that day was to evaluate that TSCM firm to see if they were carrying out the task correctly. At that time, I was working as a subcontractor to another firm and happy to take the work. My genuine love of rugby made me even more curious about the IRFU's situation.

It was still early morning as I made my way across the road to the hotel. There I introduced myself to team manager Ger Carmody. Carmody had been briefed by Phillip Browne on who I was, but I asked him to keep my true purpose a secret until such time as I was fully on top of the situation. The team meeting that day was to take place in two large adjoining rooms on the ground floor – a counter-surveillance nightmare.

With several windows facing directly out onto public spaces and multiple doors leading into the rooms, any half decent operator could bug the room with ease. The IRFU had appointed a security guard for the day to prevent people entering the meeting rooms. In fairness to him, he was only one guy, not sufficient to cover all the entrances to the rooms. Carmody directed me to the meeting room and informed me that the team, including Eddie O'Sullivan, would be along in the next hour. The TSCM operator was already on-site. As I entered the room I was surprised to see hotel staff still milling around the place, setting it up for the day's meeting. A TSCM sweep should always be carried out with just the search team present, otherwise it is quite pointless. Then I saw the 'TSCM operator' wandering around the room with a handheld radio receiver, one that could be easily bought for a few hundred euros at any gadget shop. My professional instincts were now awakened. These guys are known in the trade as 'magicians' because they walk around like they're waving their magic wands. It all looks very impressive to the untrained eye, but to those in the know it was blatantly obvious that this guy was no former police or intelligence officer, and lacked the training and experience of one.

No physical search of the room had been carried out. Not a single power or data socket had been removed. No furniture was searched and no patrol of the external spaces had been done to identify possible listening posts. This was a complete joke. Any device that was in the room would remain undetected if it was switched off until after this guy left. His sweep was complete within forty minutes, which is impossible. A team of two would have taken at least 2–4 hours to complete a sweep of the main room. Worst of all was that the room was never sealed after the sweep, so anyone could have entered afterwards and left a bug behind.

The Ireland team began to arrive and I recognised many of the greats, from the playmakers of O'Driscoll and O'Gara to the giants of O'Connell and Horgan. I had watched these men play many times over the years but today was strictly business on my part. As they began to file into the room, I got together with Ger Carmody and the security guard. It was decided that I would cover one entrance door, while the security guard covered the other. The other doors would remain locked. Roving patrols would be conducted intermittently. It wasn't a great plan but it was the best we could come up with, given that I had none of my own equipment to hand. As the day progressed, one thing became very apparent: just by hanging around the lobby of the hotel during the intermissions between the team sessions, one could gather a lot of information and gossip – everything from their drinking plans for that night to tactics that they had just been discussing. 'Loose lips sink ships' was obvious here.

It was time for me to report back to Phillip Browne. My opinion was that he was wasting his time and money with the current TSCM firm. They simply didn't know what was required to carry out a correct TSCM operation. But even more so, the IRFU had a serious information security problem. My recommendation was a full review of their current practices, procedures and physical security systems. Producing that report would involve tracking down who had carried out the previous leaks and recommendations on how to prevent future breaches. For the time being, Browne was much more interested in how the information was being leaked as opposed to who was doing it.

So began the tedious process of an information security review. First on the agenda was a test to see if I could bypass the security to get into the IRFU HQ and gather information that was openly lying around the place. I waited until everyone was at work in the building. Yes, at work! I made my way to the underground car park and to the entrance door of the building itself. The magnetic lock linked to the card reader on the door had been mounted on the outside of the door instead of the inside. I used a screwdriver to remove the outer plate, killed the power to the lock and walked in. From there I made my way up to the level where Phillip Browne had his office. His door was secured by an electronic card reader, but his PA's office next door wasn't. With no one in that office now, I strolled in unchallenged and began to flick through the diary on the desk. There I noted dates, times and names of meetings that Browne was scheduled to attend. From there I moved to a room next door where player information, including salaries, was openly on display. I now knew how much Paul O'Connell was earning. As I walked around the building that morning, picking up information as I went, not one single person asked who I was or what I was doing. I left by the front door, smiling at the receptionists as I went past.

The following night, I entered the building to carry out my own TSCM sweep of several offices in the IRFU HQ. Phillip Browne and his PA were the focus of the operation but the IT and telephone systems also had to be checked. I completed the job over a period of two nights and formulated a full report of both the TSCM sweep and the information security review. However, it was still the previous leak that fascinated me the most. After much investigating, I concluded that the room at the Shelbourne

Hotel had not been bugged, at least not in the true sense of the word. Proceedings may have been recorded on a mobile phone, or a similar device, by someone in the room at the time. Simpler, and far more likely, a copy of the minutes of the meeting may have been leaked to the media. I wished my brief had been broader, enough to fully track down the perpetrator, but Phillip Browne had been clear on that – he only wanted to know how the previous leaks had happened in order to prevent future security breaches.

'So, gentlemen, I will leave you with a final warning. The next investigation conducted by this organisation concerning press leaks will be carried through to its completion. We will identify the person or persons involved, and the appropriate disciplinary action will be taken. Before this meeting began, I carried out a full sweep of this room. Furthermore, I will be carrying out a live TSCM operation while this meeting is in progress. If anyone so much as turns on a mobile phone, I'll know about it.'

I doubt that any of these men had been spoken to in this way since they had first sat on the committee. And they didn't like it. Some of the looks I was getting were less than pleasant; in fact, they were downright hostile. When the meeting was over, I thought that would be the end of my involvement with the IRFU, but I was asked to give one final briefing to the newly appointed IRFU head coach, Declan Kidney.

Kidney had secured the post and was a popular choice with the rugby fans, if not with all the committee members. The IRFU is, like all sporting organisations, political in its own way. Some members preferred one candidate over another and if their man wasn't chosen then they were hoping for disaster. By now I had a good grasp of the IRFU and its mechanisms, and I knew who was who in the organisation. I met with Kidney and some of his newly appointed team in a meeting room at IRFU HQ. Officially, the briefing was to inform them of dangers involving information security. Unofficially, it was to tell him that not all his enemies were outside the walls of IRFU HQ. His pragmatism impressed me; he knew full well he wasn't flavour of the month with everyone and that some couldn't wait for him to cock up. Over the next few years, Kidney would lead Ireland to a series of victories including its first Grand Slam since 1948. But in the end, just like his predecessors, the IRFU ended up calling time on Kidney's reign.

Prior to publication of this book, I was approached by two former members of the IRFU committee at a rugby function. I was asked not to publish this chapter. Read into that what you will!

Chapter 7

Refusing Bribes

I wondered how many deals had been struck here over the decades – decided over a pint and a grubby handshake or by a brown envelope passed under the table to the right person – all to keep the wheels of Irish industry rolling. The Doheny & Nesbitt bar is located on Baggot Street, within spitting distance of the Dáil and every major company headquarters in Dublin, and how I wished those walls could talk. This pub is one of the oldest in Dublin and is frequented by politicians, lawyers, journalists and the high-flyers of modern-day Irish capitalism. Its cosy snugs and partitioned seating are perfect for hushed conversations. The thought of planting a few bugs of my own in this place crossed my mind. It had been an innocent enough invitation: a quick pint after work. It had come at the request of one of the companies bidding on a tender for a major security refit at a large Semi-State company in Dublin. Little did I know I was just about to be offered my first ever Celtic Tiger bribe!

By now I was well established as both a security consultant and a TSCM specialist, and between the two I had an extensive and very profitable client portfolio. I had been a subcontractor to this Semi-State company on a few previous projects, but this would be my first direct contract with them. I worked directly with their national security team and found them both professional and easy to deal with – not always the case in corporate Ireland. The project involved a major overhaul of headquarter security, CCTV and access control systems. The ageing building complex and listed status of some of its areas made for a challenging project. The fact that it was still a fully functioning workplace made it even more so. As project consultant, my job, with the help of the security manager, was to design the new system, write the technical specification, conduct a tender review, then project-manage the installation and finally sign off upon completion. It was a major project, valued at between €400,000 and €500,000. With that would come the annual maintenance contract for the successful company, which wasn't a figure to be sneezed at even by Celtic Tiger standards.

Part of the pre-tender process was to walk each of the bidding companies through the company HQ in Dublin. Any questions they had about the location of devices or about the technical aspect of the tender would be answered then. It also gave them the opportunity to work out equipment and labour costs for their bid. One of the companies tendering was Priority Security (not their real name), one of Ireland's largest security firms. My contact, David, was an affable, good-humoured guy and this was my second time escorting him around the building as he finalised his company's bid for the upcoming deadline for tender submission. It was late in the day, almost home time for us both as we finished up the second tour of the complex.

'Fancy a pint?' he asked casually.

'Sure, why not?' I replied. I couldn't think of anything better. It was a habit I had gotten into while in Australia: a quick drink after work to help ease the tension of the working day. But now for me, it was no longer just one drink; more often than not, it turned into a bender.

We headed to Doheny & Nesbitt where he called the first two pints, and we engaged in all the usual small talk – family, sport and weather – until it finally came around to the tender process.

'What do I need to do to win this tender?' he asked.

At first I assumed he was referring to the technical aspects of the process, so I replied somewhat naively, 'Well, your own proprietary system more than meets the minimum requirement in the tender, so you have no issues there to worry about.'

He chuckled softly. 'No, I mean what do we need to do to get you on our side? How much?'

It was instantly obvious that I was very taken aback by what he was suggesting. I wasn't even sure if he was suggesting what I was thinking.

'Don't worry. This is how things are done here. We will probably win the tender anyway. This is just an insurance policy. You know, just to be sure. No one will ever know. For a project of this size, five grand is the norm. Cash. No problem.'

What the fuck was going on here? This was the 'norm'? I got up from my chair, left my half-finished pint on the table and said, 'Tell you what I'm going to do. I'm going to do you a favour and forget this conversation ever took place.'

As I walked away he didn't seem in the slightest bit concerned. I doubt it was the first time he had offered a bribe, but it was probably one of the few times it had been turned down.

I left the bar and headed towards the Shelbourne Hotel where I popped in for a drink, more to steady my nerves than anything else. As I sat at the bar, I mulled over my options: I could ignore what had just happened, but that didn't sit well with me, and it could well come back to bite me in the ass at a later stage. My other option was to contact the security manager at the Semi-State company and report the entire episode. I decided on the latter. I dropped him a quick message requesting a meeting the following morning at their HQ.

I didn't sleep well that night. I wanted to get this off my chest as soon as possible, in case my professional integrity would come into question. I arrived at the HQ at nine o'clock the following morning and told the tale in full to the security manager. The reaction was not what I was expecting.

'I wondered how long it would take them to approach you. I was made the same offer last week, just not as subtle. And just in case you are wondering, no, I didn't accept. Don't worry it's all been noted, but unfortunately it's par for the course here.'

'Does this now exclude them from the tender process for this project?' I enquired, clearly concerned with how the tender process would move forward.

He simply sighed and replied, 'Afraid not. If that was the case, 90% of the companies in Ireland would be excluded from all tender processes.'

He seemed almost weary of the whole system, but at least I was off the hook for any wrongdoing. The tender process would continue. I thought that this would be the end of the subject of bribes with this project, but I was wrong.

The process had been narrowed down to three companies, including Priority Security. Like most tender processes, it did not come down to price alone: the tender was weighted. This involved considerations such as technical specification of equipment to be supplied, ability to deliver and company reputation. These and other elements were all taken into account as part of the decision to appoint the successful company. In the end, Priority Security came in at almost half the price of the other companies, and that just couldn't be ignored. I had my doubts that they fully understood the technical specifications in the tender documents, but once the contracts were signed they would be legally obliged to fulfil all aspects of the tender. When I considered the costings I had presented to the company to facilitate their budgeting for the project installation, my concerns became even greater. They were nowhere near that figure, and both I and the Semi-State security manager expressed grave concerns. We met with Priority Security at the Semi-State HQ to formally sign the documents. They were delighted. It was a major coup for them to secure such a large and high-profile sale. I took my contact David to one side at the end of the meeting and said, 'I will hold you to every word in that tender specification.' I had learned to write tender documents in Australia, and, more importantly, I had learned how to tie people up in knots with them. I was certain that Priority Security was about to learn a very costly lesson.

And it didn't take long for them to run into trouble. Within weeks they were behind schedule, mainly because they didn't have enough manpower on-site to handle the size of the project. There were other issues, too; for example, they hadn't allowed for the fact that much of the installation work would have to be done by night. These were working offices, so running cables and fitting sensors while people were at work just wasn't an option. This had been clearly flagged in the tender, but it seemed this guy from Priority Security had not taken note or maybe believed that it just wouldn't be enforced. They were wrong. I had written the tender and I planned to keep to it. It was now becoming serious. Routine quality-assurance inspections of the installation had identified that some of the equipment specified on the tender had not been installed. Some of the access control doors required two power supplies, in order to allow for additional security should an emergency evacuation of the building occur. These had not been costed into the job by Priority Security and represented a substantial additional cost. The control system was also not capable of carrying out some of the functions specified in the tender. All of this would have a serious impact on the cost of the project for Priority Security. It was time to call them in for a formal meeting.

At the far end of the canteen in the Semi-State company HQ, we all sat around a table – the Semi-State company security manager, Priority Security's project manager for the installation, their chief technician and I.

'So what's the hold-up now?' I asked, and waited for the usual list of excuses to come forth. I sat and listened patiently before reminding David that the tender document had clearly stated what was required for the installation.

What I was about to hear next, to this day, is the dumbest thing I have ever heard uttered at a formal meeting where minutes were being taken: 'The tender document is just something we sign to win the contract; we don't read it,' David blurted out.

He seemed genuinely shocked that he was expected to adhere to the document. The meeting was immediately called to a halt, and it was then that he realised how much trouble Priority Security was in. It would also have repercussions for him personally. Someone's head was going to roll, and it looked like it was going to be his. That evening David called me, asking me to meet him the next morning. He sounded desperate and so, after checking with the Semi-State company, I agreed.

He had aged ten years in twenty-four hours. We had arranged to meet at a coffee shop near Ballymount. I got there an hour early and worked away until he arrived. As I watched him approach, I couldn't help but feel sorry for him. This was a man whose job was clearly on the line.

'Before we start, everything we say here will be relayed to the client,' I said. I wanted that clear from the outset.

'How much do you think we are in the hole for?' he asked quietly.

'At least €100,000 I think. Depends on how hard the client wants to push.' It wasn't the answer he wanted to hear from me, but I was giving him the best-case scenario.

'Any room to manoeuvre at all? I'm looking at the sack here,' he pleaded.

I was prepared to advise the client to allow some leniency on certain items but only if Priority Security pushed to get the project back on track and finished on time.

'One of our senior managers wants to meet with you to try and resolve this,' he added, brightening up a little as he said this.

I think he must have been under the illusion that meeting a senior manager would impress me. It wouldn't.

'No problem, set a meeting at the HQ and I'll see him there,' I responded.

He hesitated a little. 'We were hoping to catch you for a breakfast meeting, just to iron out the technical details that are outstanding.'

Meeting them alone didn't bother me because all of this and the contents of any meeting would be relayed back to the client anyway. We arranged to meet at the Red Cow Hotel.

Over breakfast, both men seemed very focused on what actually had to be done in order to get things back on track, and I was happy with the way things were going. The meeting then took a decidedly dodgy turn. David excused himself from the table, leaving his manager and myself alone at the table.

'We really need to get this project back on track and repair our relationship with the client. Obviously you know that cost has become a problem for us. If there was any way you could help us with that, we could put more work your way.' He hadn't looked up from his plate yet. 'We have contacts in another Semi-State company that's rolling out a national security installation programme. Everyone could be a winner.'

I didn't respond. By now David had returned and the conversation turned to other matters. When breakfast was finished, the senior manager called for the bill, but I purposely made sure that the waitress took my card for payment. I wanted nothing from this meeting and that included a free breakfast. As his manager took his leave, David elaborated on Priority Security's relationship with this other Semi-State company and how I would fit in if I played ball on the current contract.

The setup was as incredible as it was corrupt. This other large Semi-State company had a national security manager whose technical knowledge of security systems was very limited. This left him with a problem: he couldn't write a technical specification for a tender process. However, rather than do the sensible thing and hire a security consultant to do it, in step Priority Security, and in particular their sales manager, to the rescue. Unofficially, of course!

'I occasionally visit his home and help him write up the tenders. The great thing is, it's written in such a way that we are in the best position to win it. It would be much better, though, if we had the right "independent" security consultant writing it instead, obviously making sure we still come out on top,' he quipped.

This was unbelievable. A major Irish Semi-State body was at the heart of a corrupt tendering process, and they were openly telling me about it. I made it clear that I wasn't interested, but I was curious to see how many of this Semi-State company's security tenders had been won by Priority Security. From the signs I had seen outside many of this Semi-State's premises around the country, it was a considerable number.

Priority Security went on to complete the project at the Semi-State HQ. I wish I could say that was the last I saw of corruption in Irish industry, but it wasn't. It seemed that everyone was riding the gravy train brought on by the Celtic Tiger. Corruption had reached epidemic levels in Ireland, and even at the time of writing this book, scandals are still surfacing that show how far greed and ineptitude reached into Irish society.

Chapter 8

Military Grade

It's the moment that every TSCM operator waits and hopes for, and now I could hear the sound of the Dixie Chicks singing 'Sin Wagon' over my headphones. There was an eavesdropping device in the boardroom, and I had to find it. I first checked the spectrum analyser to see what frequency the sound was broadcasting on. Unusually, this was operating at a frequency I wouldn't normally have associated with a commercial job, but nonetheless it was there. The initial excitement of finding the device was now replaced by concern. The fact that I was able to hear music on the iPod I had placed in the meeting room meant that the device was permanently on, not a freak anomaly on the spectrum analyser. Of greater concern was that I had not picked it up on either my fingertip physical search or with the handheld NLJD detector. This one was either well-hidden or I was getting sloppy. I hoped it was the former. I was told this was just a routine sweep of the boardroom and offices. There had been no indication that the clients were concerned about potential threats from commercial espionage. Still, this is what I was paid to do. It was my second night on this particular job and I had just discovered that RBS bank, one of Ireland's leading financial institutions, was under covert surveillance.

The biggest ever operating profit for a Scottish company, £10.3 billion, was announced by Royal Bank of Scotland in autumn 2007; this was the equivalent of £1 million per hour. In the space of seven years, the company had borrowed billions to acquire twenty-six other companies, including the acquisition of Ulster Bank in Ireland in 2000. It had grown from a small regional bank into the fifth-largest bank in the world. Chief Executive Sir Fred Goodwin ensured RBS bought every bank and financial institution it could when they entered the market. Many of these purchases made little or no economic sense to the rest of the marketplace.

At fifty, Goodwin was another rising star in the financial world, the Scottish equivalent to Ireland's David Drumm. Just like Drumm at Anglo Irish Bank, Goodwin was determined to see RBS become a giant in world banking. Despite concerns by some of RBS's senior staff that the bank was becoming overstretched, Goodwin's iron grip on the company prevented anything from stopping his master plan. In 2007, 'Fred the Shred', as Goodwin was now known following his cost-saving measures at Clydesdale Bank, seemed determined to outbid rivals Barclays Bank for the Dutch bank ABN AMRO, no matter what the cost. £49 billion was the final price tag for the Dutch bank – a sum which was later described by Gordon Brown as 'irresponsible'. This huge amount was spent despite there being a run on Northern Rock in the UK a few weeks previously; it made little sense to many of those analysing the market. But Sir Fred didn't stop there. His list of acquisitions continued to grow. I think he believed too much of his own media hype; he had been named

Forbes magazine businessman of the year. It wasn't only on acquisitions that Sir Fred was spending the bank's money; corporate sponsorship was also at the forefront of the RBS model, with deals with Six Nations Rugby and Williams Formula 1 top of his list. I think the most outlandish sign of RBS's spending was the bank's new HQ on the outskirts of Edinburgh, built at a cost of £350 million. The building came complete with its own Tesco, Starbucks, swimming pool and 500-seat restaurant. This coupled with a £17 million private jet was causing many eyebrows to be raised.

I had researched all this before the job, but I hadn't thought that it would be relevant until now. It turns out that RBS's current troubles might very well be relevant to my sweep. I had two issues now: I needed to find the device and then find out who had planted it. I had arrived at RBS HQ on St Stephen's Green at around midnight the previous night. I had already been in the large office building during the day, where I was shown which offices had to be swept. As usual, I had waited for things to quieten down around the Green before entering the building. I drove my van around to the rear underground carpark, reserved for the executive members of the bank due to its small size. The security staff manning the underground garage were expecting me, although, as always, the name and company they had on their list certainly wasn't mine. I unloaded my equipment and made my way to the executive floor. The location of the offices was a TSCM nightmare. Many overlooked the Green, which made it easy for a radio or laser-targeting device to be used. The main boardroom was worse; it was overlooked by an adjacent hotel, meaning anyone could check into a hotel room and use it as a listening base for covert eavesdropping devices that had been planted. The sweep for covert cameras that I conducted on the first night had turned up nothing. The physical search was long but routine, and I had not come across anything untoward. By the end of the second night, I had finished my search with the NLJD detector and was just starting my first sweep with the spectrum analyser when I got the hit on the main boardroom.

Finding this device wasn't going to be easy. I had already missed it on my fingertip search and on the search with the NLJD detector. This indicated that the device was professionally inserted. The boardroom was large with windows lining one wall looking over the adjacent hotel. The blinds were already closed, so I could work without being seen. I moved quietly into the boardroom, the Dixie Chicks still blaring over the iPod. I was conscious that the device I was looking for was still active. Any noise I made could alert the would-be 'spy' that I was looking for the device, and scare them into switching it off. This made my job twice as hard. I also wanted to keep as many options open as possible for the client as to how they wanted to deal with this. I stood for a few minutes scanning the room again for anything out of the ordinary but still nothing seemed conspicuous. I picked up the handheld NLJD detector and set it to its most sensitive level; this meant that I would pick up a lot of spurious signals and I would have to work through each one individually. I was acutely aware that I needed to be out of the building in the next few hours, so the pressure was on. Having searched through the furniture, floor, power and datapoints, I now turned my attention to the ceiling again. It was a plasterboard finish with access points located throughout – a good place to plant a device. I began scanning each access point within a radius of an arm's length, about as far as I reckoned a tall man could reach. The first two turned up a blank but the third was giving off a constant signal. The access point looked like it hadn't been tampered with, but I decided to take a look anyway. I quietly unfolded my ladder and opened the hatch. With just enough room to squeeze my head and arms through, I began to sweep the inside with my torch. Nothing stood out at first, then I spotted it and my heart sank.

Fuck! What do I do now? This wasn't a commercial-grade device, certainly no off-the-shelf eavesdropping bug. The tiny device, no bigger than a match box, contained both a radio transmitter and a GSM SIM card, leading to a tiny microphone protruding through a pinhole in the plasterboard ceiling. It was connected into the lighting circuit giving it an unlimited power supply. This device could be dialled into remotely to activate or deactivate it. It was well disguised and looked just like any part of the normal lighting circuit. To the untrained eye, it would go totally unnoticed. In truth, I was raging with myself because I had missed it on the first two passes. There were two possibilities here. Firstly, it could have been planted by an ex-law enforcement, military or intelligence officer who had built the device themselves. Secondly, there was a government agency of some sort keeping tabs on RBS. For me it was the latter. The device was just too advanced to have been constructed by an individual without access to the right components. This device was designed to be listened into on a permanent or semi-permanent basis. That's a lot of man hours for a rival firm to put in place. And finally, its construction looked very familiar to me. I don't think that this device was of Irish origin, as in not from the Irish authorities. It bore all the hallmarks of the devices that were used in Northern Ireland, only better. This was constructed by a British agency, which one I didn't know. I had been sitting at the top of the ladder looking at the device for twenty minutes and still couldn't come up with an answer. There is an unwritten rule among TSCM operators, depending on which side of the fence you were, to not remove, report or comment on devices planted by law enforcement agencies. For starters, there is the moral aspect, but more importantly, you don't want to piss any agency off. You never know when you might need their help. Hindering an official investigation can also have very serious legal ramifications. Besides, I had many friends in both Irish and British agencies who might well have planted this device.

It was time for me to leave for the night anyway, so I put everything back as it was, and packed up my gear. As I headed for home my mind was spinning. I had been hired to do a job by the client, RBS, but I believed the device I found was military grade – that meant law enforcement, something I wasn't prepared to tamper with. It was early morning and the first of the traffic was making its way into the city centre as I headed out to Malahide along the coast road. It was too early for a drink, much to my disappointment, as I could really have done with one. I didn't sleep at all that day, knowing that I had one last night in there to complete the job and file a report. That night, I completed the sweep with the spectrum analyser and was more focused than I had been for a long time. I was now suspicious of even the slightest signal that seemed out of place; I was chasing shadows, really. I found nothing more and, finally satisfied, left the building. My mind was made up. I knew what I was going to do.

My reports always followed the same format: listing what sweeps I had carried out and where, recommendations to enhance security and InfoSec, and finally any findings in relation to illicit activity. The report on the RBS headquarters in Dublin was no different. My findings reported the discovery of an unusual signal, listing its frequency and which room it had been discovered in. I recommended that security around the boardroom be increased and that steps should be taken to isolate the room from electronic signals. It was there I left it. Given the current state of the banking crisis I did not want to hinder any potential investigation against the bank. But RBS's troubles were far from over.

RBS was horribly exposed to the sub-prime mortgage crisis, meaning the loans they had purchased were worth only a fraction of what RBS had paid for them. I think the description by David Buik, partner at city firm BGC Partners, said it best:

> [The downfall of RBS was] all down to a degree of arrogance the like of which you will never see again in your lifetime. Fred Goodwin is a megalomaniac. RBS never had a chance to digest anything they bought and so they've never delivered shareholder value. It's a combination of relentless greed and an inability to deliver shareholder value. They were buying companies when their share price was at its peak, rather than when shares were at rock bottom, and they clearly got involved with things they just didn't understand.

At this point RBS needed to raise £12 billion from its shareholders to fill the gaping hole in its finances – another record set by the bank, but not a good one. When the banking crisis finally hit, RBS had no choice but to accept a British government bailout. Their assets were now worth a fraction of what they had been.

In October 2008, the British government announced a bailout for RBS and other banks, including HBOS. Chief Executive Fred Goodwin left RBS, saying he was 'sad' to be going. Later he would offer a 'profound and unqualified apology for all the distress caused' by the bank's collapse. In April 2009, Goodwin was described as a 'benefit scrounger' and a 'cataclysmic failure' at the bank's annual meeting where 90% of investors failed to back the remuneration report in protest at his £703,000 a year pension. In an effort to appease the growing anger, Goodwin agreed to give up £200,000 of his annual pension. In 2012, Goodwin was stripped of his knighthood but no further action was taken against him.

Perhaps I should have reported the device I discovered, but given the fact that £1.58 billion of taxpayers' money would have to be pumped into RBS Ireland to save it, I am still hopeful, if a little naively, that a conviction may yet be brought against those at the top for the reckless way in which they behaved. RBS and Fred Goodwin were no different to our own Irish banks. In the end, it all came down to one word: greed.

Chapter 9

A 'Pen' for Seán Sr

I wiped my sore and tired eyes, glad that this project was almost finished. I had been looking through the large magnifying lens for hours now, carefully working on the covert listening device that had been ordered from me. The electronic circuitry was very basic, not in the least bit complicated. It was the size of the components that made the construction difficult. Normal commercial or store-bought pens with listening devices fitted to them tended to be much bigger, chunkier pens, allowing for the circuitry to be fitted much more easily, but that wasn't an option for the device I was now constructing. The pen had been supplied by the client. It was slim and expensive. Everything, including the built-in audio-storage device, microphone and activation button, had to fit into it seamlessly. It didn't matter. I had built smaller and more complicated devices during my time in the military. It was just time-consuming. The finished product would not only have to work as a covert audio-listening device but also as a fully functioning pen. Unfortunately, there was a possibility that the device would have to pass more than just a cursory glance. It could be subject to a proper TSCM sweep prior to its use, hence the reason I was being so careful. Very little of this device was made of metal, so it wouldn't be picked up by a NLJD detector. It would take someone in the know to deconstruct it and find the hidden device. The 'pen' was now capable of picking up a conversation from about 15 feet, more than enough to capture what the client wanted. The internal filters would clean up the signal to provide crystal-clear recordings for later review.

It wasn't the device that I would have recommended, but the client was adamant about what they wanted and, after all, they were picking up the tab. It was time to test the device. I made my way to a coffee shop across from my Malahide apartment and ordered a coffee. The place was busy with the nouveau riche of the Celtic Tiger era, everyone trying to display their wealth and outdo each other. To me it all seemed so vulgar, but it was the way of things in Ireland now. I placed the pen on the table in front of me and twisted the top 90 degrees clockwise. The device was now active. Most commercial 'spy pens' use the clicker at the top for activation and deactivation, but that is too obvious for a trained eye. Twisting the pen is more subtle and less conspicuous. Later, after listening to the recording back at my apartment, I made some adjustments to the sensors and filters to ensure the best possible audio output. The luxury pen fully suited the person that would use it. I wasn't supposed to know, but I had just built a covert listening device for one of Ireland's wealthiest families – the Quinns. It was September 2008.

The 164th-richest man in the world in *Forbes* magazine's 2008 Rich List, Seán Quinn Sr was the wealthiest man in the history of the Irish state, with a personal fortune of €4.7 billion. Born in Derrylin in Co. Fermanagh, Quinn came from humble beginnings. It was in 1973 that his meteoric rise to such wealth began, with a £100 loan to set up his gravel business. Washed sand and gravel were sold to local builders and farmers by Seán Quinn Quarries, but it would not take Quinn long to branch out into other industries. Cement and glass manufacturing were next on his list, all of which were a success. Next came the establishment of the Quinn Group of companies. This would be Seán Quinn's master stroke. His interests now spread into the insurance sector through Quinn Insurance, which offered incredibly low deals on various insurance policies during the period of the Celtic Tiger, undercutting his competitors and shaking the Irish insurance market to its core. With his insurance company expanding into the UK market, by 2008 it was Ireland's second-largest insurance company and represented almost half of all revenue raised by the Quinn Group.

Now being hailed as 'The Mighty Quinn', Seán, like so many other Irish, decided to move into the property development and management business. With property, in particular hotels, in fourteen different countries involving over seventy companies all falling under the umbrella of the Quinn Group, his portfolio was substantial. Estimated to be worth over €500 million in 2008, the portfolio, which according to the BBC generated $22 million in annual rental income from the Kutuzoff tower block in Moscow alone, was ever expanding. Hotels throughout Eastern Europe, a large shopping mall in the Ukraine, and the Belfry Hotel, the home of the Ryder Cup, were among the properties to increase the Quinn Group's prestigious portfolio. Like so many other high-flyers of that era, Seán Quinn Sr seemed to be able to do no wrong.

Whether through some foresight or just by chance, Seán Sr handed ownership of the Quinn Group to his five children, Seán Jr, Brenda, Ciara, Aoife and Collette. While all of them had worked for the company at some point, Seán Sr continued to run the company throughout its most successful period. This exchange of ownership would be the subject of much controversy in the coming years.

I knew none of this when I had been approached with this current job, but I did know that it wasn't going to be run-of-the-mill. The request had come through a third party, who worked for another security firm that I had dealt with before. Our arrangement was quite simple: any TSCM or counter-espionage work that came his way he would pass on to me because he didn't have the knowledge or the equipment to do it himself, and for his trouble he got a 15% finder's fee. He was beating around the bush as we sat over a pint in Dundrum town centre, something he never normally did.

'Get to it, Karl. I haven't all day,' I pressed.

'I have a client that needs a listening device. Something top-shelf, but they need it at short notice,' was his eventual reply.

'Forget it, Karl. I'm not interested, not my thing and you know it. Besides, you don't need me for this. Buy something online. It will do the job.' I dismissed him offhandedly. I hated when people wasted my time, especially people I knew.

Karl, however, was a money man and saw the opportunity in everything. 'Come on, Seán. It's a good earner and I know you love that sneaky-beaky shit,' he urged.

Thing is, the fucker was right. Counter-espionage is always interesting but espionage, getting a device in where it shouldn't be, by-passing all the security in place and making them look like fools, well, it gave me an incredible rush. He must have noticed my slight smile as I momentarily reminisced about the good, or bad, old days in Northern Ireland. He knew he had a bite. I'd give him ten minutes to sell it to me.

His pitch didn't exactly have me clambering to take on the job, but what he wasn't saying did. My questions were the same as those I would have posed for any would-be covert eavesdropping operation: what type of conversation was I bugging, a private conversation or a full meeting with many different people? Where would the meeting be held: an office, boardroom, bar, restaurant or out in the open? Would I have to deal with background noise, other conversations or environmental noise? What would the distance be between the listening device and the target conversation? Was the client male or female? This made a difference as to where I might hide a device. What did the client hope to achieve by bugging the conversation? And, of course, what type of device did they have in mind?

He answered all the questions I posed with the same answer: 'I can't say.' And so my reply to his request was, 'Tell your client to hire an amateur then, and stop wasting my fucking time.' With that I got up to leave. As I did, he grabbed my arm indicating for me to sit down again.

'Let me speak to the client and see how much I can say and how much I can't. Give me ten minutes?'

I nodded in agreement and he made his way out to make a phone call. As I awaited his return, I mulled over the operation. It was a classic, clandestine, commercial operation, where the client wanted excellent results but gave you sod all details. Details are what allow a good covert technician to build a device suitable to the task, without them you might as well hang up your boots.

Karl returned full of beans. 'I've been told I can elaborate a bit further for you.' He said this as if the client was doing me some kind of favour. I couldn't have cared less; I didn't need the work. The conversation would be a private conversation involving only a few individuals. It would be held in an as yet unnamed hotel, most likely in an open foyer or perhaps a private meeting room. The client needed a clear recording of the conversation – all details of what was being said would have to be picked up. Now that I knew what I was dealing with, this operation would be no problem. 'One other thing, the other party involved may be aware of an attempt to "bug" the conversation and might take their own precautions against it.' He was now grinning from ear-to-ear knowing full well he had me. Whatever the device was, it could be subject to a TSCM sweep if the client was searched before the meeting.

'OK. I recommend we build a remote listening device into a laptop bag or wallet. We'll keep it switched off until it gets past any search team, then switch it on and record it remotely. I can set up a listening post close to the meeting point.' I knew from the look on his face that this wasn't going to be acceptable.

'Sorry, Seán, but the client wants any recordings of that meeting kept to themselves, so a remote recording with anyone else listening in is not an option.' With that, he slipped a slender, gold and very expensive pen across the table to me. 'It needs to be fitted to this and with the recorded storage built in. And the client needs it by tomorrow.'

It would be a challenge but one I would take on. I was intrigued by the whole thing. The potential of trying to get a device past a sweep team had the adrenaline rushing – sad but true. This is what I had spent most of my career doing.

I decided that my fee would be €5,000. Considering the work I would have to put in, the short timeframe and the level of expertise to build the device, I thought it was fair. It was, in truth, just a number I had plucked from the air! This job was a first in many ways, but the most surprising was that the client wanted to haggle on price. Given who the client would later turn out to be, I couldn't help but laugh. Having started work on the device that afternoon, Karl called. Clearly embarrassed, he informed me that the client wanted some wriggle room on the price. Negotiating down my price was new for me, so I agreed to knock off 10% for a cash payment.

Once the device was tested and ready to be handed over, I planned to meet Karl at a café just off Merrion Square in the heart of Dublin city centre. I was there ahead of time, as always, and when Karl arrived he was in high spirits. That was about to change. He slid the envelope containing my fee across the table, less his cut of course, but I didn't take it. I took the pen from my backpack but didn't immediately hand it over.

'Who's the client, Karl? And more importantly who are they bugging?' I was deadpan, no jokes this time.

'Seán, I can't. This is too big. If it gets out, there will be serious repercussions,' he insisted.

I took the pen and placed it back into my backpack, slid the envelope back across the table and smiled. 'I'll have the pen back to you in an hour in its original state.' I knew I had him over a barrel. If the meeting was today then the client wouldn't have the time to source a second device, and that would not be good for Karl either.

'Seán, you can't breathe a word. Seán Quinn is meeting with someone from Anglo Irish Bank today. The bug is an insurance policy about some deal or other. That's all I know.'

I believed him. I knew of the Quinn companies from my time in Northern Ireland where they were a well-known company and large employer and this presented me with an issue, one that Karl had no knowledge of. Anglo Irish Bank and a number of its executives were clients of mine, mostly in the form of counter-espionage. By now, I knew that something wasn't right at Anglo, and I would soon be taking out insurance policies of my own, so who was I to stop anyone else from doing the same. I was confident that there would be no TSCM operation in place that day. I was Anglo's go-to man at this stage, and I hadn't been tasked to perform one. I told Karl as much as we exchanged 'gifts'.

I could have left it at that and walked away but I wanted to know more. What was the issue between the Quinns and Anglo Irish Bank? It was September 2008, time to do some digging, and I knew just the man to start with. One of my many contacts was in CAB (Criminal Assets Bureau), without doubt Ireland's most successful law enforcement agency. If there were any rumours floating about, either about the Quinns or Anglo, my contact would have it. That was the way of things in Ireland: information was currency. I could pick up the phone and call any one of my contacts within An Garda Síochána and get information contained on their PULSE information system or from within their own intelligence networks. Oftentimes, it was simple things like giving a car registration and finding out the owner, but on other occasions I needed more than that. It was, of course, a two-way street. I often provided my sources within the force with sensitive information about those that I was working with and for. The old boys' network was alive and well in Celtic Tiger Ireland. Data protection and the legality of such exchanges never came into it. Not for the first time, my contacts came up trumps.

It turns out that this hadn't been the first such meeting between the Quinns and Anglo Irish Bank. The clock was ticking for both parties now. The Quinns had got it wrong, spectacularly wrong. CFDs (Contracts for Difference), a term that would become synonymous with the Quinns and their relationship with Anglo Irish Bank, would be the downfall of not just both parties but the entire Irish banking system. Seán Quinn Sr and his family had built up a substantial shareholding in Anglo Irish Bank – nothing unusual in that given that the bank had been so successful during the Celtic Tiger. Remember Anglo had the title of the 'Best Bank in the World' in 2007. The complex structure of CFDs was the financial instrument that Quinn used in building up his now substantial stake in Anglo Irish Bank shares. A CFD was basically taking a bet on the share price, as opposed to buying the shares outright. This meant Quinn didn't have to spend as much money as he would have buying the shares in the normal manner. The big difference with CFDs was that as long as the share price was going up, Quinn was on a winner, but if the share price were to fall, Quinn could lose an awful lot of money. Using the CFD method of buying shares, Seán Quinn Sr was able to build up a substantial stake in the company, almost 25%, completely unbeknownst to both the board and the executives in the bank.

The first meeting between Seán Quinn Sr and Anglo Irish Bank CEO, David Drumm, was on 11 September 2007 at the Ardboyne Hotel, Navan. It was here that Quinn disclosed that he owned almost 25% of the bank through CFDs. The bank needed to unwind Quinn's shareholding in the bank, and they needed to do it quietly. It was now feared that Quinn could no longer fund the losses on his CFD bets, as Anglo's share price continued to fall over the following months. If he were forced to dump his shares onto the market, it might undermine confidence in the bank and cause the complete collapse of Anglo Irish Bank. In order to cover his losses on the CFDs, Seán Quinn Sr borrowed heavily. However, the so-called St Patrick's Day Massacre in March 2008, when Anglo shares dropped by almost 30% in a single day, made his situation desperate. With great hesitation, Quinn agreed to cover his losses by buying 15% of the 25% CFD holding, and the remaining 10% would be sold on the open market. This was easier said than done. No one wanted to buy the 10% of Anglo shares on the open market. Anglo Irish Bank then approached a group of wealthy clients and extended them loans totalling €450 million to purchase the shares. This group became known as the Maple 10 and included developers Seamus Ross, Gerry Gannon, Gerry Maguire, Paddy McKillen, Joe O'Reilly and Paddy Kearney; businessman Gerry Conlan; auctioneer and developer Brian O'Farrell, and builders Sean Reilly and John McCabe. David Drumm, Willie McAteer and Pat Whelan would later be convicted of offences in advancing the loans, but there is no suggestion any of the ten investors did anything wrong. Loans to the value of €2.34 billion were also extended to Patricia Quinn and her five children for the same purpose.

In May 2008, as the Anglo share price plummeted, a loan of €288 million was taken by Seán Quinn Sr from Quinn Insurance to fund the endless demands for cash to cover the Anglo CFD losses. That same September in 2008, Lehman Brothers filed for bankruptcy and the global financial crisis accelerated. Quinn's troubles continued in October 2008, when the Financial Regulator penalised

Quinn Insurance with a record €3.2 million fine. Seán Quinn Sr, who was personally fined €200,000, stood down as director and chairman of the Quinn Group. The fines were related to the loans from Quinn Insurance to cover the CFD losses. By March 2010, the High Court had put Quinn Insurance in administration, sparking widespread protests from staff and supporters. In March 2011, Anglo Chief Executive Mike Aynsley stated in an RTÉ interview that Quinn companies would not remain in the family's ownership.

It was at this stage that the alleged plan was put in place by the Quinns to place their overseas properties beyond the reach of Anglo Irish Bank. The following month, Anglo Irish Bank appointed a share receiver over the Quinn Group to recover €2.88 billion worth of loans owed by family. New directors were appointed by the receiver, removing the Quinn family from the empire they had built from nothing. But the Quinns were not going to give up without a fight. In May 2011, Seán Quinn's wife, Patricia, and the five children sued Anglo, claiming loans of €2.34 billion advanced in 2007 and 2008 were 'unenforceable', as they were made for the 'illegal objective' of manipulating the stock market to support the bank's share price. In June 2011, the High Court issued orders restraining the dissipation of international property assets by the Quinns. For Seán Quinn Sr the news kept getting worse as he was hit with separate debt awards of €1.74 billion and €416 million by the commercial court in November 2011. By 2012, even his attempts to file for bankruptcy were thwarted in Belfast, and he was forced to file for bankruptcy in Dublin instead.

I do not claim to understand the complexities of the Quinn v IRBC case, but I do have an understanding of commercial espionage. Given what I know about what was happening at Anglo Irish Bank at the time, an insurance policy by anyone dealing with them would have been a smart move. If that meeting at Buswells Hotel in Dublin was bugged using the device I provided, why hasn't it been produced to date? There are a number of possible reasons. The bug was discovered before the meeting and therefore couldn't have been used at all; I find that highly unlikely. A malfunction or operator error in activating the device could be a possibility. It's quite possible they bottled it beforehand and decided not to take the risk of being caught red-handed with such an illicit device. The dark side of the espionage world tends to raise more questions than answers, and always will.

Chapter 10

Precautions and Paranoia at Anglo Irish Bank

'It's what the client wants, so just design it, price it and deliver it,' the architect growled at me angrily.

The discussion had been going back and forth, not just at today's project management meeting but over the past couple of meetings. He was now getting annoyed at my failure to comply with David Drumm's wishes.

'This is way over the top. It's simply not required. You're talking military grade here. The cost will run into six figures,' I continued to argue. My job was to deliver the best possible solution for the client, and that included value for money. I was the expert here but, as is often the case at these meetings, egos tended to outweigh experience.

The client was requesting armoured communication cables into his office and those of other senior executives, along with some of the meeting rooms and boardrooms. I had designed many such systems over the years, but all of them were for military installations. Hell! MI5 HQ in London had armoured cable, but only because it might be subject to a physical attack on its communications. That was it! The penny finally dropped! The combination of all the other shadowy work I was doing for this client unbeknownst to everyone else in this room was now making sense. Armoured cable is used as a preventative measure against a physical tap being placed into a communications network. It prevents side leakage from the cables contained within it, so the armoured cable would have to be dug up, cut into and then a physical tap put onto it. This is time-consuming, very obvious and takes a certain amount of skill to achieve it clandestinely. There is only one type of organisation that has both the lawful right and the expertise to do this, and that is a law enforcement agency of some form. Anglo Irish Bank, my client, and in particular David Drumm, knew the bank was in trouble. It seemed to me he had known for quite some time, and now they were prepared to do anything to keep it quiet, including preventing any regulatory or investigating body from accessing their communications network. It was all coming together for me now. The trouble was, in my own small way, I had been helping them in their subterfuge.

I had been involved with the design of Anglo Irish Bank's new headquarters in the heart of Dublin's trendy Docklands since the very beginning. It was to be a beacon of excellence, and with that a demonstration of just how pampered the Irish banking system and its employees really were. The complex included individually climate-controlled workstations for the traders and had not one but two gyms – the senior executives could not be seen sweating with their juniors, after all. The staff restaurants and open foyers would put any 5-star hotel to shame. The executive top floor boasted a rooftop bar and private dining room and kitchen – perfect for entertaining developers and politicians alike. It was everything that was wrong with the Celtic Tiger. But it was all fur coat and no knickers, as my mum would say. I was part of the security design team, and everything about it would be state-of-the-art. The access control systems included end-to-end encryption, thus making an unauthorised breach almost impossible. There was so much CCTV covering the building that it would be impossible to move anywhere without being seen. But it was the executive levels and communications rooms where most of the security was focused, and now I knew why. This all made sense for a bank, but not for a bank that didn't actually hold any cash.

From the outset, I had encouraged the design team to focus on InfoSec, as that was where the bank's main vulnerability lay. However, my advice fell on deaf ears, and more and more focus seemed to be fixed on preventing people entering the building, in particular the executive levels. The lifts to the executive levels were to be access-controlled, again a move I would not have taken much notice of had I not known the more illicit work I was doing on behalf of the bank and its executives.

By now there were signs in the market that the boom would soon become bust. It had started in February 2007 when the markets were briefly rattled by fears over US sub-prime mortgages, but they soon recovered. This was only a few weeks after one of my many sweeps at Anglo Irish Bank. I believe those at the top of Anglo Irish Bank knew then what was coming. The first fall in property prices since the start of the property boom were recorded in March 2007, and the following month Morgan Kelly on RTÉ's *Prime Time* forecasted a collapse in property prices and massive bank losses. The beginning of the real credit crunch began in June of that same year with the securities and debt markets coming under intense scrutiny by analysts. Despite all these warning signs, the then Taoiseach, Bertie Ahern, responded to Morgan Kelly's analysis as follows: 'cribbing and moaning is a lost opportunity. In fact, I don't know how people who engage in that don't commit suicide.'

The run on Northern Rock bank in the UK on 14 September 2007 saw images of customers queuing to get their cash beamed across the globe. Anglo Irish Bank raised €2 billion in covered bonds in October and posted €1.24 billion in profits in November 2007. But by 2008, the US sub-prime mortgage crisis reared its ugly head once more and the riskier property investments were finally exposed. In the now-infamous Anglo tapes, David Drumm said in January 2008 that he was prepared to burn bondholders by buying the bank's debt at 60–70 cent in the euro. In February 2008, Northern Rock was nationalised by the UK government. But it was March 2008, when US bank Bear Stearns was rescued from the brink of collapse and Anglo Irish Bank shares fell 30% in a single day – the St Patrick's Day Massacre – that the cracks finally started to show, not only in Anglo Irish Bank but in the Irish economy as a whole. It was at this point that a colleague on the project management team pointed out that this would be a great time to buy shares in Anglo, as the shares were bound to recover in time. If only he knew what was really going on. Share prices continued to fall over the coming months while lending to the Quinn Group rose – a course of action that would eventually lead to one of the biggest court cases in the history of the state.

My more covert work at Anglo Irish Bank had become more and more bizarre. I was still being tasked by the bank to carry out TSCM sweeps at an alarming rate, but that wasn't the only unusual aspect of the work. It was becoming increasingly obvious to me that many of the senior executives at Anglo were keeping the TSCM sweeps I was carrying out on their behalf to themselves. None of them wanted the other high-level executives to know what I was doing for them. It was now a case of rats leaving a sinking ship and every man for himself. Paranoia at Anglo Irish Bank hit levels I had never experienced before either in the commercial world or even in the world of military intelligence. I wasn't even sure if I was being paid by Anglo or individual executives themselves for much of the work I was doing. In fact, much to my own detriment later, many of the bills weren't paid at all. I wasn't too concerned at that time, however. After all, they were a bank, so I'd eventually get paid, wouldn't I?

I knew something was seriously amiss when I was asked to do a full sweep of Anglo's backup data site. For anyone who works in the area of commercial counter-espionage, this is a highly irregular request. Due to the level of cybersecurity that companies, in particular financial institutions, invest in their IT networks, illicit penetration of such sites is almost impossible. And yet, despite my recommendations to the contrary, here I was heading to this off-site data centre located in a high-security facility on the outskirts of Dublin. I arrived and went through the rigorous security checks to gain entrance to the building. I was escorted by a security guard to the area containing the Anglo Irish Bank equipment. It was a state-of-the-art facility, containing row upon row of climate-controlled cabinets in which the data servers were stored. I did a complete sweep of the system, looking for any software or hardware bugging. None was found. It was utterly ridiculous that a rival commercial firm could plant an illicit device in such a high-security facility, and I didn't believe a word of the story that the facilities manager at Anglo had spun me. Some of those at the very top of Anglo believed they were under surveillance by some form of regulatory or law enforcement body, and I was there to ensure that anything that may have been planted was found and removed. Even paranoid people have enemies, as the saying goes, and that was what was behind all this. The next time I saw David Drumm he was not the same man I had seen when I first began working for Anglo Irish Bank. Gone was that confident, almost brash figure that stalked around the Anglo HQ, sending people scuttling out of his way. By now I had carried out sweeps of every part of his life: office, car and home. He was a shadow of his former self. The weight of the world was on his shoulders, and I finally knew why, and he wasn't the only one.

And then it happened. The message was short and to the point: the following morning's project management meeting was cancelled and the bank would be in touch with further instructions. The phone started hopping. Everyone was ringing around trying to find out what was going on, but it was obvious to me that the new Anglo Irish Bank headquarters would never be finished, at least not by Anglo. Many of us were left holding the can, with bills unpaid. For me it was even worse. I had been working for the bank in two capacities, and now the invoices for both were outstanding. My mind was now racing with worry, when people within the bank who would normally take a call from me at a moment's notice were suddenly unavailable. No form of communication was being replied to. All the TSCM work from Anglo had dried up overnight, and I was about to learn a very harsh business lesson. On 15 September, the US bank Lehman Brothers collapsed, filing for bankruptcy in New York and causing turmoil in the global financial system. Two days later, Anglo Irish Bank executives met a Central Bank official. Anglo wanted a €7 billion emergency loan. On 29 September 2008, the Irish government took an overnight decision to guarantee the banking system by covering customer deposits and the bank's own borrowings to a total of €440 billion. As late as 3 December 2008, Anglo Irish Bank was still trying to convince the market that it was still profitable and solvent in its annual results. Two months later, in January 2009, Anglo Irish Bank was formally nationalised. It would report a loss of €12.7 billion – the biggest corporate loss in Irish history.

To be perfectly honest, I didn't give a fuck about all that. I was primarily concerned about the money I was owed and my own business. My hands were tied for now. The queue of people looking for money from Anglo was a mile long, and I was very much to the rear of that queue, but I was prepared to play the long game. I did, however, get the opportunity to add to Anglo's woes: I tried to make it easier for any investigation by ensuring they knew where all of Anglo's information was kept. A mate of mine from CAB called me on the morning that the bank guarantee was announced. He was calling on behalf of one of his own contacts in another anti-fraud unit.

'Seán, anywhere other than their offices that we should be looking?' said the voice down the phone.

I knew who 'they' were without asking, and I also knew where he might have a chance to pick something up, where Anglo officials might not have had an opportunity to clean house yet. 'Their backup site. It might not be sanitised yet.'

He didn't even say goodbye as I gave him the address, such was the rush to get hold of anything that they could use later against Anglo and its executives.

Despite all the money that Anglo Irish Bank and individual executives within that institution had spent on TSCM and commercial counter-espionage, it was their own internal system that had caught them out. I'm not sure if that's what they call irony, but it sure is bloody funny. It was in the now-infamous Anglo tapes that each of the Anglo executives accused of wrongdoing would hang themselves. These were the internal calls on Anglo's own telephone system that were recorded. Most, it is assumed, knew they were being recorded as part of standard practice, but as with most things over time, one tends to not so much forget about them as become comfortable with them. It was something that had never really crossed my mind. My TSCM operations were there to find illicit eavesdropping devices planted by those outside of the company or on behalf of someone outside of the company.

The tapes would demonstrate the true disdain that those at the top had for the Irish people. In one call, Drumm was heard describing Financial Regulator Patrick Neary as 'f**king Freddie f**king Fly' and the Central Bank as a 'shower of clowns'.

'You can't take it off f**king Freddie f**king Fly down there, the Financial Regulator, because it will appear on the balance sheet,' he went on to say. Drumm, it seemed, was unaware that he was being recorded and spoke about getting money from the Central Bank. 'We'll be saying, "Yeah, a stress because HBOS were f**king sold and Lehman's went bust and f**king Bank of America f**king took over Merrill's and other f**king non-normal things happened. We need the f**king loan because we are running out of money."'

His arrogance on these tapes was beyond measure as he continued, 'I'm going to keep asking the thick question:

"When, when is the cheque arriving?'" he said, adding, 'if we say it in their language, nothing will happen. You have it, so you're going to give it to us and when would that be? We'll start there.' He would go on, 'If they don't give it to us on Monday they have a bank collapse, if the money keeps running out the door the way it has been running out the door.'

For me the tapes would put the final piece of the puzzle into place. I now knew where the institutional paranoia had come from. The sweeps and the additional security measures all made sense, but Drumm wasn't the only one caught with his pants down by the Anglo tapes.

The recordings had also focused the spotlight on CFO Matt Moran and John Bowe. Their description discussing a planned meeting with Ewen Stevenson of Credit Suisse was most colourful, as they openly discussed plying him with alcohol before asking him for €5 billion. They seemed to be not in the least bit concerned that their calls might well be recorded. It was the deal with the Irish Life and Permanent (ILP) that would ultimately save or sink the bank.

Despite all the precautions and paranoia, there would be consequences for those at the top of Anglo Irish Bank. Charges were brought against Seán Fitzpatrick, Tiarnan O'Mahoney, Bernard Daly and Aoife Maguire, all former employees of Anglo Irish Bank. Fitzpatrick was charged in relation to the €450 million in loans given to investors to buy shares in Anglo. The other three were charged with conspiring to defraud the Revenue Commissioners. The use of the €7.2 billion in temporary loans from ILP to Anglo Irish Bank saw charges brought against Denis Casey of ILP and William McAteer and John Bowe of Anglo Irish Bank. These loans made the bank look far healthier than it actually was. Further charges were brought against McAteer and Fitzpatrick with regard to fraudulent loans and finally, David Drumm was charged with two counts of deceiving depositors and investors into believing that Anglo was healthier than it actually was at the height of the crisis.

Had Anglo Irish Bank and its executives been up front with me from the start about what was happening and who they were trying to avoid, my approach would have been much different. I may not have taken on the job at all, but if I had, then an internal recording system would have been launched out the window on day one. Instead, like many such clients, you are led down the garden path with cover stories that hinder you. In this game, the TSCM operator doesn't really care about the backstory. We don't judge, but we do need to know what we are fighting. To be honest, I'm delighted the internal recording system wasn't part of my remit. Without those recordings, no one would have grasped the sheer contempt these bankers had for the banking system or for the ordinary people who would have to fund the bailout. Each of the men mentioned above would ultimately face trial, although some were harder to get before the courts than others. Anglo Irish Bank will go down in history as the bank that cost the Irish taxpayers €34 billion and plunged the country into more than a decade of recession and a generation of debt. It was no longer the 'Best Bank in the World'.

Chapter 11

Evasive Action

The opulence of the 5-star Westbury Hotel in the heart of Dublin city centre would be the setting for my first interaction with this client. I sat in the gallery area on the first floor waiting for the gentleman in question to arrive. It turned out that he was either too busy or too important to drag himself away from the other side of the hotel to see me himself, so his PA arrived instead. He handed me the mobile phone and sat down across from me, looking over his shoulder as if he was expecting some spy from a 1980s cold war movie to apprehend him.

I took the laptop from my bag, booted it up and connected it to the mobile phone. The software would do its thing and seek out any malware or spyware that might be secreted in the mobile phone's software. It would take a while, so I ordered myself a coffee. There was no small talk while we waited. I couldn't be arsed and to be fair neither could the guy opposite me. After ten minutes, the laptop pinged, indicating the search was complete. It had come back with a clean bill of health. The job wasn't complete, though. I removed both the battery and the SIM card from the handset and gave the device a visual inspection, looking for any physical evidence that the handset had been tampered with. Next came the handheld scanner that I carried in my bag. It was small and discreet, yet was sophisticated enough to locate any illicit hardware that might be secreted into the phone. Satisfied that the phone was clean, I reassembled it, placed a small seal over the handset and handed it back. It was only now that he spoke.

'Mr Lynch will be in touch about the rest of the project,' he said, and proceeded to saunter off across the gallery.

The first part of a much larger project I would carry out on behalf of one very paranoid Philip Lynch of investment group One51 was complete.

Philip Lynch was born in 1946 in Innishannon, Co. Cork. He was educated at Hamilton High School and went on to study accountancy and economics. His first job was as a sales rep for Odlums, but he soon moved to managerial roles at R&H Hall. In 1983, rivals IAWS poached him to be its CEO. There, Lynch led the evolution of IAWS from a heavily indebted agricultural wholesaler to a conglomerate with a multimillion-euro turnover. Lynch set up One51 after leaving IAWS, and he used it to buy stakes in NTR, ICG, Greenore Port, IFG, Datalex and many more. Almost €200 million was put up by investors to further One51 investments.

Irrespective of how successful a businessman he was, his approach to my work was a bit of a joke, unfortunately. This was apparent as I sat in my vehicle outside his offices. It was broad daylight, in the middle of a working day in the heart of Dublin: not exactly the time to be carrying out my type of work. Still, this was the job, and it was the way he wanted it done. On the plus side, it was only the telephone system I was sweeping, so I didn't need much equipment and it wouldn't take too long. I unpacked my toolbox and the flight case containing my telephone analyser and headed towards the main door. The upstairs office was open-plan and had five or six people in it – not ideal. As far as they were concerned I was there to do some routine maintenance on the telephone system, but anyone with half a brain would know it was more than that. I started with a physical search as always, checking the access panels and handsets for signs of tampering, taps or bugs. All came up clean, and then it was time to use the analyser. Now everyone in the office was staring at what I was doing. I couldn't wait to get out of there, but I still had to search the control room and PABX. With the location searched and the UV seals put in place, I left. After I sat back into the hired van, I called Lynch's PA.

'Job done, all clean,' I said.

'Great, I need our offices at Carlingford Lough done next,' he whispered.

This guy was really starting to annoy me. It wasn't the fact that I had to get my ass up to Carlingford Lough, I quite fancied the drive, but it would be a daytime operation again.

'Listen, mate. Can we not do this at night or at least at the weekend? I like to stay out of the way, be discreet, and tearing a place apart in the middle of the day is about as discreet as a baby elephant.' I think he got that I was slightly pissed off.

'OK. It could be done Saturday, I suppose. Just the phone system again.'

What was with this guy and the phone system? I had tried to explain to him that the phone system was only a very small aspect of a TSCM sweep. I wasn't looking to get any more money out of him or anything; it was just my professional opinion. Of course, there was a chance that this guy knew something he wasn't telling me. In fact, that was highly likely, but I still put it down to the fact that he had been watching too many spy movies.

The drive up to Carlingford Lough was quite pleasant and as I arrived at the two-storey building at least I had some background on this job. The sign on the gates read 'OpenHydro': the tidal energy firm of which Philip Lynch was a director and One51 was an investor. They were bidding on a contract which involved installing up to ten tidal turbines at the Paimpol-Bréhat (Côtes d'Armor) site, in north-west France from 2011. There were four other bidders involved for a contract worth €20 million. Now this did make sense – a contract of this size would make it well worthwhile eavesdropping on the competitors' bid prices and the technology it planned to use. Either piece of information would enhance your bidding strategy.

This time there was just one person on-site to allow me access to the building. Once inside they left and let me go about my business. The job was straightforward and turned up nothing, but at least I wasn't falling over people while trying to get the job done. As I drove back towards Dublin, I received a panicked phone call from a colleague.

'Can you organise a bodyguard for Philip Lynch?'

Now this was a strange one. What in God's name did Lynch want with a bodyguard? He was hardly top of anyone's hit list.

'When does he need it by and what's the problem?' I asked, more nosey than concerned.

Apparently, Lynch was involved in the refuse business through one of his many business interests and had now fallen foul of some very individuals, who he was afraid would do him some injury. I was chuckling away to myself as the details were being relayed to me over the phone. I'm not sure what one lone, unarmed bodyguard was going to do against a club-wielding mob, but I made some calls anyway. I had just hung up on my contact, all the arrangements made, when I received a further call to stand down. The panic was over. It seems Mr Lynch had somewhat overreacted. Either way he was on my shit list, as I had just called in a few favours to get him someone quick-smart.

The next call from Lynch's PA detailed the next part I was to play in his increasingly paranoid life. As I pulled the car into the garage, I was trying to piece everything together. To date, I had swept all of Lynch's telephone systems including his personal mobile, and now he requested to have his car swept. Usually, this indicates that the client has very specific concerns, but despite my requests for further information, I was told little else. Sweeping a car involves a lot of work and it also involves taking the car pretty much to pieces. The Mercedes in front of me was not going to go through that ordeal, however. I had been told in no uncertain terms that the car was not to be damaged. Lynch's driver, who had delivered the car, had been adamant about that. I wasn't sure if that was coming from Lynch or from him, as he clearly loved that car. So I would once more be hampered in carrying out a thorough job by Lynch's restraints. I started with a fingertip search, or at least as best as I could. A search of a vehicle without removing the internal parts is very difficult; there are so many places to secrete an illicit device, especially if a professional has planted it. It would really be down to the electronic search equipment to find anything untoward. I started with my small handheld scanner, cursing the car manufacturers for having installed so many gadgets in the vehicle. Each one set off the alarm on the scanner and required me to investigate each hit. This was hugely time-consuming. My body ached by the time I got out, having been twisted into all shapes in order to search every part of the vehicle. Next I placed the transmitter/receiver into the car, put my headphones on and sat back to listen for any feedback from the iPod I had positioned in the car. Finally, I searched the undercarriage, engine and boot for any tracking devices. Despite the sweep coming up clean, I was curious as to why I had suddenly received so much work from Philip Lynch. The truth would soon come to light.

In July 2011, Philip Lynch was ousted as chief executive of One51 after the board terminated his contract. Chief Financial Officer Alan Walsh was appointed interim chief executive with Executive Director Michael Long as his deputy until a successor could be found. The company announced that it had been 'considering succession for some time' and paid tribute to Mr Lynch for 'his significant contribution to the development of the company'. Lynch, on the other hand, said he was 'disappointed'. It was known that talks about Lynch leaving had been ongoing for some weeks. He made it clear that he had been forced out. His removal came only three weeks after One51 secured refinancing of €200 million and approved a new strategic plan for the investment company. The plan was needed as the company had struggled with its share price falling from €5 in 2007 to just 90 cents in July 2011. Now all of Lynch's paranoia was obvious, if a little amateurish. The revolt against Lynch had started the year before when Gerry Killen, a less than satisfied One51 shareholder, led the 'Campaign for Change at One51' against Lynch. Lynch still maintained that despite the drop in share price, the company was in 'great shape' and the share price 'did not reflect this value'. Lynch went on to say that a 'divisive and personalised campaign' against him had left the company in a 'vulnerable' position, and the campaign had 'served to destabilise the company and erode further its perceived value'. All this had been going on while I was doing TSCM work for Lynch. He was no fool and had been taking precautions.

The collapse of the One51 share price left many top businessmen and companies with multimillion-euro losses, with some of Ireland and Britain's biggest dairy co-ops losing more than €100 million off the value of their shares. The Kerry Group took the biggest hit with a loss of €40 million. Some of Ireland's biggest names felt the hit also: beef baron Larry Goodman saw a €9 million loss in his stake; former Esat Telecom Chief Executive Barry Maloney's shares lost €1 million in value; property developer Bernard McNamara's shares were down by €800,000; former Irish Nationwide Building Society boss Michael Fingleton's stake fell by almost €300,000 and golfer Pádraig Harrington's shares were down by €80,000. But this wasn't to be the end to the saga – far from it. In February 2016, Philip Lynch was awarded a summary judgement for €1.5 million against his former employer, One51, by the Court of Appeal. He had sought payment of €1.48 million due to him under a patent income scheme. His first success in this case had come in 2012, when the High Court in Dublin had instructed his former employer, One51, to pay him €1.4 million due to him from share and loan notes held by Chandela Nominees Ltd. Now the Court of Appeal had upheld that judgement in his favour.

The shareholder revolt with One51 and the subsequent court case were not the only reasons that Lynch had to be paranoid; he had one more tangle to be wary of, and that was a loan from AIB bank.

In February 2007, AIB bank had extended a loan of €25 million to Mr Lynch, his wife, Eileen, their four children – Judith, Phillipa, Therese and Paul – and developer Gerry Conlon. The loan was issued to fund the purchase of 86 acres at Kilbarry, Co. Waterford, where a shopping centre and retail development were planned. It was then valued at €80 million, and after development and sale, a profit of €21 million would be realised. The end of the Celtic Tiger and the resulting property crash would soon put an end to those plans. The Lynch family would now claim that they did not have to pay those loans back. They believed the loans to be non-recourse: in other words, the lands for which the loans were made to purchase could be repossessed by the bank but they could not be personally pursued by the bank. AIB claimed, however, that the loan organised by Conlon was given on a full recourse basis. In December 2011, the courts ruled against the Lynch family, saying it had failed to show that AIB had been negligent in how it dealt with them and that they should repay the loan. The legal costs for the case were expected to run into the millions, and the land in Waterford ended up being worth €3 million. Despite all Mr Lynch's evasive actions, they weren't enough to rescue him from his woes.

Chapter 12

From Russia With Love

I was out of my depth. I hated admitting it, but I was. I knew the building was under covert surveillance, but, somehow, I just couldn't find how they were doing it. The fingertip searches I had conducted had turned up nothing, and not even the very sophisticated and expensive electronic search equipment that I was using had found anything. I took solace in the fact that the people I was up against were the best in the world at this, and had been for over fifty years. Whatever they had planted or were using to listen in on the conversations in this building would be state-of-the-art. They were ingenious in their methods of hiding illicit eavesdropping devices. I couldn't help but admire them, and they had well and truly stumped me on this occasion. For the first time in my career, both military and commercial, I would have to admit defeat. Had I known who my adversary was from the start, I would have turned the job down. No one is foolish enough to take on the Russians!

The security officer at Cork Airport was about to pop the locks on the flight cases that contained my TSCM equipment. I had hoped to avoid this situation. While the equipment wasn't illegal, it attracted unwanted and sometimes unanswerable questions. As he opened the case, I could tell from the look on his face that he had no idea what he was looking at. Time for a little bluff!

'Can you tell me what this equipment is please, sir?'

'EMF scanners. We use them for buried fibre-optic cables,' I replied, without so much as a pause.

'Yes, I thought that alright. No problem, sir. Carry on.' He now looked good in front of his colleagues and, besides, the equipment posed no threat to anyone.

We were heading to London to carry out a TSCM operation. I hated these jobs – not knowing what you are getting involved in before showing up for the job. I hadn't wanted to take the bloody job in the first place, but Rob, the guy with me, didn't want to turn down the €10,000 plus expenses for three days' work. More than that, I think he just wanted three days away from his missus.

The initial contact had been made through an Irish IT manager working at the company's London office. I had no idea who the client was or had any background on why they wanted a TSCM search carried out. I had arranged to carry out the sweep over the three nights of the weekend. The client had been adamant about that. No one was to see us going about our business. I wasn't even sure if three nights would be enough because I had no idea of the scale of the project. As we flew over the Irish Sea, I sat thinking about the job. It had puzzled me why a UK-based firm would hire an Irish company to carry out a TSCM sweep for them. There were plenty of good firms in the UK – ex-military guys of the highest calibre. It was much more expensive to drag us across the pond to do it. As soon as we landed at Gatwick, we grabbed a taxi and headed for the hotel I had booked in the centre of London. It was all on the client, so we stayed at the Washington Hotel in Mayfair. Rob was in his element; it was like he was on holidays. It was his first time on a TSCM sweep and he was in for a bloody shock if he thought it was all tea and biscuits! We checked in and immediately hailed another taxi to take us to the client's premises in the heart of the City of London business district.

The building was what you would expect for an office in the centre of London's financial sector: a striking piece of architecture overlooking the Thames. No expense had been spared here. We walked into the impressive foyer and approached the reception desk. We didn't know what company we were looking for. We just had the name of an individual. They were obviously expecting us, as we had only just sat down when we saw two men approaching us. Tall, with pale skin and a shock of red hair, there was no doubt that this guy was Irish. He was accompanied by an equally tall and very muscular black man. He introduced himself and his companion, the head of security.

'I half expected you guys to abseil on to the roof,' he laughed, as we followed him through the security checkpoint and into the building proper.

We took the lift to the fifth floor. The plate next to each floor gave the name of the company; we landed at 'Clarkson Shipping Brokers'. It didn't ring any bells with me.

'I'll take you to see our CFO. He'll brief you on what's been happening and what he wants done.'

With that we were led to a small meeting room and served coffee while we waited. And wait we did; almost two hours later the CFO graced us with his presence. I was far from impressed by this.

'Right, so I guess you're wondering why we got the Paddies in to do the job? Well, I don't trust any of the local firms. They still might have some allegiance to the government. You know how it goes.'

He was clearly oblivious to my military background, so I let him waffle on.

'We are in a court battle at the moment, and the other side seems to know everything we are planning before we even get to court. My concerns are that one of the meeting rooms or offices may be bugged. So, I'd like you guys to search them over the weekend when no one else is about. The two boys will accompany you while you carry out the work.'

It seemed plausible that there was some kind of surveillance going on, but I pressed him a bit further. 'Are the other side capable of carrying out that level of espionage?' I asked.

He burst into laughter. 'You tell me. It's the Russians!'

Russians? Fuck! Was he talking a company or the state? It didn't really matter; it was all the one, really, especially when it came to international dealings. He passed a list of rooms he wanted swept across the desk.

'You need to be finished by Monday morning,' he said, and with that he upped and left.

In the taxi on the way back to the hotel, I had it out with Rob. 'We should walk away now. I want no part in this,' I said, angrily.

But he was adamant. 'We're here now. Let's just do it and be on the first plane back on Monday, payment in hand.'

I reluctantly agreed but decided to do a bit of background research as soon as we were back at the hotel.

In April 2007, Clarkson, the world's biggest shipbroker, was sued for $54 million by two of Russia's biggest shipping companies: Sovcomflot and Novoship. Legal action was initiated at the High Court in London by Russian state-owned oil tanker company Sovcomflot. Among the list of defendents in a second action brought by another Russian state-owned carrier, Novoship, was Clarkson. Clarkson was potentially on the hook for up to $21 million and the news of the pending legal case sent its share price to the floor. The action against Clarkson related to commissions paid to third parties during business dealings with the two Russian state-owned companies, dating between 2001 and 2004. The word from Clarkson was that they would fight the legal action all the way. As soon as the legal proceedings began against Clarkson, one of the companies' non-executive directors, Martin Watson, resigned due to a potential conflict of interest. Not good news for Clarkson. So this was what it was all about. Great! A state-owned Russian company against me and a novice TSCM operator! My fee should have had an extra zero on the end of it.

We arrived at the Clarkson offices just before midnight, TSCM kit and tools in hand. The list of offices to be swept was extensive and we would need every hour available to us. We started immediately. Rob went ahead of me to remove the cover plates and datapoints, and I came behind and inspected them. He was keen and wanted to be more involved, so I gave him a few rooms to physically search. Unfortunately, he missed a few very obvious 'Easter eggs'. 'Easter eggs' are items put in place by the client to ensure you know what you are doing. It's a common enough trick, but Rob had missed them. It was my fault – I should have done it myself. We moved on, and over the three nights carried out a full physical and electronic search. Still, we turned up nothing, but I knew it was there. It was a gut feeling – something I had learned to trust over the years. But time was up and nothing was showing. I had to head back to Ireland, write the report and file it with the client. This was not how I like to leave things. Before we left, we had a quick meeting with the CFO again.

'Missed some of the gifts I left you then?' he smirked.

'Yeah, sorry about that. Rob's first job.' There was no point in bullshitting.

'I know you found nothing but are we under surveillance?' he whispered, as if he was sure someone was listening in.

'In my professional opinion, yes, without a doubt.'

He stuck out his hand, thanked me and said payment would be wired to my account that day.

The whole thing was still bothering me two weeks later, so I put a call into the client and recommended another sweep, this time by a UK-based company. They had a bigger crew than me and were all ex-military or British Intelligence. In fairness, the client didn't hesitate and agreed immediately. I contacted the new crew: guys I knew and had worked with before. They would go in that very weekend. My heart sunk as I took the call on the Saturday morning. They had made a find.

'It was in the paintings, mate. We were lucky to find it, so don't beat yourself up too hard.' He was being generous, of course.

It was brilliantly executed. The paintings were provided by an outside company, leased and changed every four weeks or so, to give the board and meeting rooms a fresh feel. A pinhole listening device (without a transmitter and with just a small USB data recorder) had been hidden behind the hanging points. The device was hidden in such a way that when the alarm from the NLJD detector went off during the sweep, it would seem as if it was the metal clips that were triggering it. When the paintings were changed the recordings would be removed and another device put in its place, giving the opposition a heads-up on all Clarkson legal strategies.

There would be further strange twists and skullduggery with this case. The High Court in London would clear Russian shipowner and businessman Yuri Nikitin of the claims made against him by Sovcomflot and Novoship (with whom Sovcomflot had now merged). The decision came after a trial spanning six months in which Sovcomflot and Novoship sought to recover approximately $850 million they claimed was owed to them as a result of the alleged dishonest actions of Mr Nikitin and others. All allegations against Mr Nikitin regarding the alleged bribery of and fraud and conspiracy with Dmitry Skarga, the former Director General of Sovcomflot, and Tagir Izmaylov, the former President of Novorossiysk Shipping Company, failed completely. Claims against Nikitin in relation to some of the commissions paid to him by Clarkson, and others, were successful. Clarkson had been ordered to pay up, their legal strategy had failed and the Russians had gotten one over on them. But the vast majority of the claims against Mr Nikitin were found by the court to be based on dishonest evidence from dishonest witnesses employed by Sovcomflot and Novoship. The court accepted that the witnesses who lived in Russia, especially those employed by Sovcomflot or the NSC group, would have felt 'great pressure' to support the claimants' case, and that the evidence from the claimants' key witnesses was 'thoroughly dishonest'. Clarkson now had a huge settlement to pay, and it had come from Russia with love!

Chapter 13

Two Weeks With 'The Don'

It was around 10 p.m. on Friday, 23 April 2010, when two armed and masked men entered the Fassaugh House pub in Cabra, north Dublin. Although the two gunmen had entered via the front door, they initially went unnoticed by their target, Eamon 'The Don' Dunne. Dunne was part of a large group, including his 17-year-old daughter and members of his criminal gang, that was sitting to the left of the door. One of the gunmen remained at the door to provide cover while his fellow hitman made his way towards Dunne. All the while a third man remained outside the pub watching for anyone that might come to Dunne's aid. No one did. A getaway driver was at the ready in a nearby car. This was a thoroughly professional hit team. As the gunman walked towards Dunne, he pushed people out of the way, yelling at everyone to get down. Nearing Dunne, he discharged the weapon. Dunne was hit several times from behind, then again as he turned, despite trying to use the lounge boy as a human shield. In total he was hit six times in the head and body. He did not survive. The killing was over in seconds and was captured on CCTV inside the pub. Moments later, the culprits were driven away at speed.

The attack was, without doubt, intelligence-led. There were two theories. The first was that one of Dunne's own gang had informed the hit team about not only the pub where Dunne was but also the exact spot where he was sitting. Dunne had attracted a lot of Garda attention in the years leading up to the attack. This was bad for business, therefore bad for his gang. The second was that an accomplice of the attackers had been sent in advance to recce Dunne's location in the pub. Either way these guys had carried out a near perfect assassination, a fact that even the Gardaí investigating the case would later admit. Despite the large crowd attending a fortieth birthday party there that night, very few witnesses would come forward to the authorities. No surprise there. Dublin's gangland would deliver its own brand of justice, as Dunne had just found out.

I wasn't sure how I felt as I read of his demise in the evening paper. I was sitting in Gibney's pub in Malahide, the very spot I had met 'The Don' almost two years previously. I had been asked to meet him by a long-standing client who had grown up with Dunne but had no connections to crime himself. I had done my own research on him, and I wasn't looking forward to the meeting. Known as 'The Don', 34-year-old Dunne ruthlessly controlled the Dublin drugs trade. Anyone who crossed him usually ended up dead. A big problem for me was that Dunne was a regular user of the cocaine he supplied. That made him highly paranoid and thoroughly unpredictable. Dunne liked to style himself on drug lord Marlo Stanfield, from the TV show *The Wire*. Dunne was from Dunsoghly Drive, Finglas, and had taken control of Martin 'Marlo' Hyland's Finglas-based drug gang after Hyland had been shot dead in December 2006. The hit was believed to have been carried out by Hyland's own gang because, ironically, Hyland had attracted too much Garda attention as well.

Dunne wasn't your typical Dublin criminal. He sat his Leaving Certificate in 1993, coincidentally the same year I did. He also ran his own business, a motor company, although this was believed to be just a front for his criminal empire. It was 2002 when Dunne first came to the attention of the Garda. He was caught in a house in Finglas with a large amount of cocaine and ecstasy. A 10-year sentence was handed down despite Dunne's attempt to fight it. Five months later, a car that Dunne was in was stopped at a checkpoint, and a bound-and-gagged man was found in the boot. No charges could be brought against Dunne because the restrained man never made a complaint. Between 2002 and 2005, several high-profile armed robberies had Dunne's name written all over them. He was also believed to be behind the murders of drug dealer Andrew Dillon in 2005 and John Daly in 2007. Daly had angered many criminals who were incarcerated in Irish prisons after he telephoned the *Liveline* radio show from inside Portlaoise Prison using a smuggled mobile phone. The resulting clampdown on contraband made life very difficult for some of Ireland's most dangerous criminals, and Daly had to pay a price. Dunne had strong links with other criminal gangs, such as the Limerick-based McCarthy-Dundon gang. He was charged with conspiracy to steal almost €1 million from a cash-in-transit van when he was arrested by undercover Gardaí at a Tesco car park in Celbridge, Co. Kildare, in 2007. This guy was not to be messed with.

The soft-spoken man sitting directly across from me in Gibney's pub didn't quite match up to the profile I had constructed.

'I'm being watched, and I need to know how to ditch the fuckers following me.'

'Who do you think is following you and why?' I whispered. As soon as I had asked the question I wished I hadn't.

'The National Drugs Unit, CAB, the Organised Crime Unit and every guard in the fucking country, but I'll take them any day over the guys who want me dead. I've already been told that my life is under threat,' he replied.

Fuck! I really wanted no part of this. 'I'm not sure what I can really do for you. I'm more technical counter-surveillance than anything else.'

It was then I saw it. Criminal kingpin or not, this guy was scared and probably had every right to be. He wasn't afraid of arrest or prison, although I dare say he would have rather avoided both; he was terrified of a bullet in the back of the head. I couldn't, and wouldn't, help this guy avoid the law, but I would try to keep him alive long enough for the Gardaí to bang him up. I could teach him the basics of counter-surveillance and personal security – all the skills I had been taught for the streets of Northern Ireland.

Over the next hour I got as much information about the current security precautions he was taking as I could. Dunne was far from stupid. He was moving from house to house regularly, wearing body armour when out and about, and he kept a circle of friends who acted as bodyguards close to him (although I think this close circle of friends may have been behind his eventual demise). He even slept in caravan parks occasionally to try and stay ahead of his pursuers. During the hour he was with me he visited the toilets about half a dozen times, and judging by the traces of white powder on his nose, he didn't have a urinary infection! I agreed to meet him two days later at the car park of the Grand Hotel in Malahide. The subject of payment had never come up. In truth, I had been too nervous to mention it. I would be happy to let this fee slide and walk away as quickly as possible.

Good to his word Dunne arrived at the hotel car park at nine o'clock. I had been there since seven o'clock, looking for anything untoward. I had told him to get the DART to Malahide station and make his way on foot to the hotel. I noted the body armour he was wearing beneath his clothes as he approached, and I scanned the vicinity to make sure no one was following him. He jumped into the passenger seat. He seemed positively enthusiastic about what he was about to learn. He shouldn't have been; most of it would be utterly boring. He even brought a notepad and pen. It would have been funny, if the situation wasn't so serious. I decided to start with the very basics.

'Did you check under your car before you got into it this morning?'

The blank stare told me he hadn't. I handed him over a pack of clear circular seals, about the size of a one-euro coin, and a UV light pen.

'When you lock the car, place one of these stickers at the opening point. Before you open the door again, run the UV light over it. It will tell you if the seal has been broken. If it has, walk away.' Next came a folding mirror that he could check the undercarriage of the vehicle with. With the recent rise of dissident republican activity in Dublin, car and pipe bombs were a very real threat.

I moved on to some tips regarding basic counter-surveillance. 'Park your vehicle a good distance from where you are staying, do a couple of walk-bys and see if there are any strange vehicles or people hanging around. If there are, leave and head for another safe house. Install CCTV at the places you stay, and get the doors and windows re-enforced. This will buy you time if there is an attack on the house.'

He was scribbling down notes as I spoke. I almost asked if he had access to a weapon but stopped myself, knowing full well that he had.

'Use mirrors and reflective surfaces to spot surveillance,' I continued. 'Vehicle mirrors, traffic mirrors and the glass in windows can all be used to spot surveillance without looking directly at those who might be following you. Retrace your steps – it makes it easier to spot surveillance, but be careful you may tip your hand and force them to do something there and then. Stop unexpectedly to read a sign or look in a window and see how the people on the street behind you act and react. Buy a cup of coffee or eat lunch in a crowded area. Longer stops make amateur surveillance easier to spot. Change your pace, and see if anyone tries to match your pace. Head to a known safe area, a place you have decided on before heading out. Once there, have a look and see who has followed you in. Always deviate from your route; never take the same route twice. Seek out crowded places if you feel like you have a tail. It's easier to get lost in crowds and you are less likely to get attacked there – too many witnesses. Change your appearance when you can – take off your jacket, put on a hat. Change your mode of travel – grab a taxi, use the Luas or jump on a bus. Turn and hide, move off your planned route and find someplace to lay low.'

To be fair, he was eager to learn and wrote everything down on the notepad he had brought along.

'Okay, finally if you believe you are under imminent threat, call the Gardaí. Sirens and blue flashing lights will scare any potential attacker off, or at least distract them for long enough for you to get away.'

Now it was time for some vehicle counter-surveillance. I started the engine and eased my way out of the car park, heading from Malahide towards Dublin Airport and the motorway. As we drove, I provided a running commentary. 'Make four right or left turns. The probability that another vehicle just happens to make the same 360-degree turn as you is slim to none. You both might make one or even two turns, but anything more means you might have a tail.' Next, I took an off-ramp and then got right back on the motorway. 'Just like before, not many people get off the motorway and right back on again. The tail is assuming you are exiting and exits with you, but you'll burn them if they follow you back on again.'

Dunne nodded intently, a slight smile now creeping onto his face. He was loving this.

'Don't get too cocky. This doesn't always work against large professional teams. A good surveillance team knows this trick and will exit the motorway the proper way. The first burned vehicle drops being the lead and radios back for another vehicle to continue on the motorway to pick you up again. To thwart this, skip exiting the motorway altogether. Stay on the motorway, and every few miles pull over to the side of the road to "smoke" or "make a phone call".'

As we drove back into the city, I began a series of stop and pull-ins. Each time we stopped, I told Dunne to note the last three digits of the first five vehicles that went past. This would tell him if the same vehicles were following him. Even a good professional team found this one difficult to work around. It had just dawned on me I was actually teaching him how to ditch a professional surveillance team – the law! It hadn't been intentional; I had just gone through what I had been taught.

Over the course of two weeks we practised all the forms of anti-surveillance I had taught him. He was quick on the up-take and more intelligent than I had initially given him credit for. Was he under surveillance? Damn right he was! Over the fortnight I spent with him, it was obvious that he was of interest to someone within the Garda ranks. I think, though, it might have been for his own safety, as much as part of any investigation. Patrols regularly passed where he was known to stay. I was strongly advising him to stay out of areas he was known to frequent. The thing with surveillance is that once you know what you are looking for, it stands out like a sore thumb, and there were several sore thumbs watching Dunne. I had advised him against having any type of mobile phone and to seriously consider leaving the country altogether. He was hugely paranoid and volatile. I was nervous in his presence, especially when he insisted on going to places I knew he should stay out of. These were neighbourhoods I wouldn't normally drive into. I'll admit that on the number of occasions he had to 'pop in' to a few such places, I was terrified. I wanted out of this. I had no intention of becoming some sort of minder or driver for Dunne and was relieved when the final day came.

'I've taught you everything I can, stick to it and you'll be fine,' I lied. Dunne was going to come to a sticky end, one way or another. I made no mention of payment. In truth, he unnerved me; he was a man living on the edge and that made him very dangerous. We were sitting having coffee at a café in Howth. As I got up to leave he slid an envelope across the table. I took it and placed it in my pocket.

'Thanks for everything. I've learned a lot. Great fucking craic too,' he laughed.

I drove until I was half way to Cork before I pulled over. Cold sweat had soaked me to the skin, such was my relief to be finished with this guy. I took a peek inside the envelope, almost afraid that it might blow up in my face. When I finally opened it, there was €12,000 inside. About twice what I would have charged him.

I shed no tears for Dunne, but he was a father of three children and the law had already sentenced Dunne for his crimes, although not all of them. There was one thing that bothered me about Dunne's assassination. Not the obvious questions of who had set him up or why, but given the level of interest the authorities obviously had in Dunne, how was an assassination able to take place at all? I realise that Garda resources are finite, and they don't provide round-the-clock protection, nor should they, but I think Dunne might have been more valuable alive than dead. I learned from my days in Northern Ireland that a turned informant is a priceless commodity, and I think Dunne was ripe for the picking. Regardless, Dunne had lived by the sword and had died by the sword, and many will feel that Eamon 'The Don' Dunne finally got what was coming to him. Very few Irish criminals live to be old men.

Chapter 14

What a Sorry Semi-State of Affairs!

As I drove towards the security checkpoint at the entrance to the vast open compound on the mouth of the river Shannon, the rain poured down in sheets, driven by the strong westerly winds coming in from the Atlantic Ocean. I was wearing the required high-visibility coat and hard hat, both sporting the company logo, and so, with only a cursory glance from the security guard sitting snugly inside his hut, the barrier was raised and I navigated my way through the checkpoint.

It was almost a mile drive from the entrance to the main control building – a huge structure that towered over the Shannon estuary. I parked my vehicle in one of the designated visitor spots and rushed towards what looked like the main entrance of the building, trying to shield myself from the freezing rain. I didn't know my way around, as I hadn't been here before, so I did what any visitor would do: I asked for directions. I was looking for the main control room and with some help from the friendly staff, I soon found it. I walked into the vast, ultra-modern control room. I stood at the back of the room looking at the bank of three massive control levers and wondered what would happen if I turned all three off. It was five minutes or more before one of the duty staff approached me, not in any way alarmed, more out of courtesy to see if he could help. As I looked out from the control room over the huge conveyor-belt system feeding coal from the ship docked at its nearby birth into the power plant, I asked, 'What would happen if I switched all of these off?'

The reply came out somewhat jovially. 'That wouldn't be a good thing. An uncontrolled system shutdown could cause major damage, months of repair work. Half the western seaboard would be without power.'

It was one of Ireland's largest generating stations, with 3x Brown Boveri turbines, controlled by the three control panels in front of me. It had three units, each with a capacity of 305 MW, leading to a total capacity of 915 MW – around 7 million MW hours per year. Coal is the primary fuel; however, it also has two Heavy Fuel Oil (HFO) storage tanks with a capacity of 50,000 tonnes. It used HFO as a backup fuel if needed. At full output, the station consumes approximately 7,000 tonnes of coal per day – around two million tonnes a year. The site includes a deep-water jetty capable of accepting vessels of up to 250,000 dead weight tonnes and a 600,000 tonne coal storage area. (A typical coal shipment was around 140,000 tonnes.) All of this information is freely available from the company's website. I, a complete stranger, had just gained unauthorised and unchallenged access into the control room of one of Ireland's largest power stations – ESB Moneypoint. Had I been only lightly armed, I could have, there and then, single-handedly held the country to ransom!

The purpose of my visit to ESB Moneypoint that day was two-fold. First, I was there to investigate the circumstances of a robbery that had been conducted at the site the previous day. The room containing the on-site ESB cash office had been broken into and the contents stolen. It was a substantial amount of cash given the number of staff members working there, and the fact that it was coming up to Christmas meant that a lot of staff had their Christmas club savings in there. It was obvious, both to the investigating Garda present that day and to me, that this had been an inside job. Only someone with knowledge of the layout of the office and the substantial amount of cash present that day could have carried out the robbery. However, there were also a large number of building contractors on-site due to a major refurbishment and they could have been involved. My second reason, and far more important, was to carry out an ethical penetration test. Ethical Penetration Testing is a formal procedure to discover security vulnerabilities, flaws, risks and unreliable environments. In other words, penetration testing can be seen as a successful but not damaging attempt to penetrate a specific information system or site – mimicking the activities potential criminals, terrorists or espionage agents would engage in with the intention to compromise a system or location.

Generally speaking, organisations conduct penetration tests to strengthen their corporate defence systems comprising all computer systems and their adjoining infrastructure. It tends to focus on the IT and cyber-hacking side of things. Under the ESB's new national security manager, a much broader approach was being taken, looking at the potential for physical breaches of security and the potential loss of information or security compromises from such breaches. My unhindered entrance into ESB Moneypoint was just one part of a major programme, each test proving to be more and more susceptible to security breaches, information loss and potential harm to the supply network. Moneypoint had a long list of factors that made it an easy target, and when I say target I don't just mean from a terrorist organisation as we might normally know it. Hijacking the control room or even one of the ships at the dock could cause irreparable damage without doubt, but an interruption to the supply network could be achieved far more easily. Moneypoint burns a lot of coal, although with great care to adhere to environmental controls, and this could attract what are now called environmental terrorists or eco-warriors. By simply climbing onto the conveyor-belt system, they could bring the power station to a halt, no weapons needed. To my utter dismay, the anti-climb fences surrounding the perimeter of the compound were fitted the wrong way round; they were now of great assistance to anyone trying to scale the fence. There was very little CCTV on-site to cover such a huge compound and there was an over-reliance on the few security guards who were on duty. Moneypoint needed a major security overhaul, just like many of the other ESB sites throughout the country that I had visited, but there was a problem with implementing such wholesale changes – the unions.

The Ethical Penetration Testing had begun at ESB headquarters in Dublin city centre a few weeks earlier. The objective was simple: to see if I could gain unauthorised entry to the building and then gather as much information as possible. I had watched the building for a number of days before making any attempt and decided that my best option would be in the evening when all the daytime staff were leaving. I had identified the rear entrance to the complex as the weakest point. Although there was a security guard on duty and a control barrier to stop any vehicles, pedestrian access was almost unhindered. This was before the installation of the new security system and things were pretty sloppy. I had a colleague with me for this job, an ex-British military intelligence officer, and this is what he specialised in. At least once every year, members of the British Army Intelligence Corps try to gain unauthorised entry onto British army military installations. All manner of inventive ideas are engaged in order to breach the security of the camp: posing as a very senior officer and trying to intimidate the soldiers on the gate; posing as the cleaning staff, or, my favourite, joining in on the back of a squad run or forced march as it returns to camp.

As the crowds started to file out of the complex, I nodded at Phil and we moved down the ramp towards the security hut. We pretended to be deep in conversation as we fought our way through the outgoing crowds. No problem, we were in! I now knew that we would go completely unchallenged for the remainder of our stay. It was the same as any corporate building: once you looked like you had the right to be there, no one would question you. Next we had to find the offices where we could gather the most damaging information. As we walked along the first-floor corridors of the building, Phil indicated towards a door labelled 'Finance' – a good place to start.

I knocked on the door, and when no reply came, I twisted the old-fashioned door knob. It was unlocked. We both quickly made our way through the door, careful to ensure we hadn't been seen. There were two offices: the first was obviously a secretary or PA's office leading into a second much larger office: an executive officer's office. Phil was like a bloodhound. He headed straight for the computor on the PA's desk, lifted the keyboard and found what he was looking for. Stuck to the underside of the keyboard was a login and password. Phil now had access to the ESB IT network, and at a very high level. While he delved into the network, I started looking at the items on the desk. There was obviously no 'clear desk' policy being enforced in the ESB, as documents were strewn all over the place. I spotted a key amongst some pens and tried it on the top drawer of the desk. Bingo! First try and I was in. What I found next was like all my birthdays coming together. Two company credit cards were in the drawer, both of which I could now use for online purchases if I so wished, but even better, stuck to the back of each on a post-it note was the PIN number for each card. Phil had finished taking notes off the system and we decided to move on. We had amassed enough damaging information from this office. It was time to see if it was a one-off or if there was a culture of such a blasé attitude towards InfoSec within the ESB hierarchy.

We made our way to the far end of the complex, to the old building that housed the most senior offices in the ESB, including those of the CEO and the CFO. I was expecting to get very little from these offices. Surely, security would be tighter here. The door at the bottom of the first set of stairs we descended opened with a slight creak; that was the only noise that came from our entry. This was a very plush office, clearly belonging to someone at the top of the organisation. We started with the basics again. We couldn't gain access to the computer network from his terminal, but what we did find would have been of use to many people outside the ESB. We found his Credit Union account statements, complete with all the information we would need to gain access to the account. His balance was very healthy, enough to warrant a tiger kidnapping. We had copies of all his payslips and bank statements. All of this would have been gold for any media outlet, or worse, it could have led to his accounts being hacked and emptied. The level of personal information available was astonishing. It didn't get any better as we proceeded through the building. Minutes of high-level meetings, diary entries and personal correspondence littered the ESB executive offices.

Phil noted with a wry smile, 'If this was the army, someone would be going to the Glasshouse for a long time.'

The 'Glasshouse' was the British military prison in Colchester, and he was right. The company executives needed to lead by example if they were to convince the ordinary workers to buy into the new security regime. We had photographed all of the damning evidence and it would form part of our report that would be delivered to the national security manager. This, coupled with results from the other penetration testing, would give him all the ammunition he needed to implement the new security framework.

Without doubt, the ESB Group of Unions was, and is, one of the strongest in the country. With that strength came a certain militancy and a 'set-in-their-ways' mindset; change wasn't always welcomed. The additional security measures to be introduced at both ESB headquarters in Dublin and the new nationwide security rollout were seen as a potential threat by the unions. I had been inside ESB headquarters a lot and noticed how union reps and officials moved around with a certain swagger; they seemed untouchable. It amazed me how unproductive many aspects of the ESB were: there were a lot of people standing around doing nothing. Each had a specific task and would only perform that one task, nothing else.

As I made my way through the compound at the beginning of the various projects I was undertaking, there were rooms I was told I wasn't allowed to enter. I ignored these orders. What I discovered in these areas was shocking. No wonder they wanted me to stay away. I saw everything from sleeping employees to groups of people playing cards, all on the company's time. When I enquired about it, I was told to leave well enough alone. It would be more trouble than it was worth to bring any kind of disciplinary action. At one stage in the post room, I found a brand-new but untouched scanner, designed to scan incoming suspect packages for threats like anthrax powder. When I asked why it wasn't being used, I was told that staff refused to be trained on how to use it. Even the security guards manning the entrances to the HQ complex and those manning the security control room were against any kind of change. It seemed very odd to me, as much of what was being introduced would make their life considerably easier. I would soon discover what was behind most of the unions' objections to the new security systems, and it had nothing to do with privacy rights.

No one at ESB headquarters clocked in or out, and no one in any of the sites I had visited around the country did either. For the unions, this was at the heart of the problem with the new security system. The new access control system would see every ESB employee at ESB HQ, and eventually nationwide, being issued with an identity card that would also act as an access control card. The new card-controlled security barriers at the front and rear of the building would only operate when one of these valid cards was presented. This access control system would record and reveal what time employees and visitors were entering and leaving the building. This could pose a problem for some employees who, let's just say, didn't always put in a full shift. The unions, despite assurances from management, feared a 'Time and Attendance' system would be introduced under the guise of the new security system. Once accepted at ESB HQ, it would set a precedent for installation nationwide. The new comprehensive CCTV system that was accompanying the access control system would show what was going on at each site, including when and where. Again, this was something unacceptable to the unions, and given what I had seen at ESB HQ I understood why. The actual operating of the new security system was being objected to by the ESB security staff, and they were supported by the unions. I really didn't understand the objections, considering the ironclad promises given by management, but a conversation with some of the management soon clarified things for me. The unions wanted more money for the introduction of any such system. Ultimately, it would be used as a bargaining tool for any future pay increments. It was just the same as their objection to using the scanner in the post room: more money was demanded for the use of any additional technology.

There was one final aspect of the new nationwide security rollout that would be resisted around the country by certain ESB employees and security installation companies alike. The new tendering process that the national security manager was trying to implement would see all security contracts centralised from ESB HQ: a national tender process. That didn't mean that one company would win all contracts nationwide but that small groups of geographically grouped sites would be awarded to one company. The difference was that these tenders would now be issued, evaluated and awarded from ESB HQ in

Dublin, thus taking power away from local managers. Up until now, each area manager would oversee the security tendering process for their area, and in many areas the same companies seemed to win the contracts irrespective of price or quality. As part of the push to get the new process in place, I had been tasked to visit a number of sites around the country. The standard of installation left a lot to be desired. At one point, following the awarding of one such contract to a company for a number of sites in the south, the ESB local manager contacted the national security manager asking for the tender process to be reissued because his preferred contractor, who had done all the previous installation work for him, hadn't won the contract. Needless to say, his request was denied.

Moneypoint, the new installation at ESB HQ, the appalling awareness of InfoSec, the trouble with the unions, and the overall lack of awareness of how important and vulnerable much of the ESB network was, became too much for all involved. The national security manager was exhausted fighting these constant battles for change, change that was absolutely needed to take the ESB into the future. The amount of time I was spending on-site trying to get the systems in place and the endless trouble with sub-contractors made many of my contracts with the ESB unprofitable. Soon enough, this coupled with the banking crisis and the collapse of the Irish economy would see my relationship with the ESB end. I had, however, learned some valuable lessons: corruption comes in all forms; change in any aspect of Irish culture is hard fought, and, with very little knowledge and resources, someone could turn out the lights in Ireland for a very long time.

Chapter 15

Was it All About the Beer?

There must have been a hundred file boxes stacked from floor to ceiling, and somewhere in amongst them an unknown signal was broadcasting. I had found it the previous night while using the spectrum analyser, and, having discounted the signals from other electronic sources in the room, I had pinpointed it to this pile of boxes. It was almost two in the morning, and the consultant who had hired me for this TSCM operation was standing beside me. He was shifting uncomfortably from foot to foot. I guess I would be too if I had just found out that one of my offices was being bugged.

I had instructed him before entering the building that night not to speak until I indicated it was safe to do so. I nodded towards the door and we both made our way outside into the car park of the Tudor-fronted 'counting house' located at Cramer's Lane in the heart of Cork's medieval city, close to the South Gate. The building was a sight to behold; you couldn't help but admire this Cork city icon. The large clock stood proud above the door telling me I had only a few hours left to sort this one out. The night-shift workers were milling around, going about their business, and they were more than a little curious as to why these two were around at such an ungodly hour. I wanted my kit packed up and to be long gone by the time the day-shift and office workers arrived, so I pushed him.

'What would you like to do about this?' The usual options were open to him: remove and tighten up security, leave it in place and try to discover who planted it, or use it to spread disinformation. His response left me flummoxed.

'Could someone other than you find it? I mean, was it difficult to locate?'

This was an interesting question. I needed to be careful here, so I replied, 'Well, I actually haven't found it yet. I just know it's in that pile of boxes. It could be secreted in any one of the files in those boxes or in the lining of the boxes themselves. If you want me to remove the device, it could take me days to search through all of it.'

Even in the darkness I could see the sly smile creeping across his face. As we stood there, a delivery truck laden down with kegs of Beamish stout rolled out through the gates of the Beamish & Crawford brewery. I had been doing this a long time now and I knew that something wasn't right – something stank here and it wasn't just the hops.

Founded in 1792, the brewery of William Beamish and William Crawford was established on a site near the Southgate Bridge in Cork, where beer had been brewed since the 1500s. But the brewery, and with it Beamish & Crawford, could cease to be should this proposed takeover deal go through. It had been already announced that Beamish & Crawford's parent company, Scottish & Newcastle, were in negotiations to be taken over by Heineken and Carlsberg in a deal said to be worth €10.5 billion. The Irish businesses would be owned by Heineken. The future at this point was unknown for the Beamish

& Crawford site. Alf Smiddy, chairman and managing director of Beamish & Crawford, was quoted as saying, 'As it will take some months to complete, it is unknown at this point the nature of the impact the transaction will have for Beamish & Crawford. Ultimately when and if the consortium's bid for S&N is successful, it will be a matter for Heineken to outline its plans for Beamish & Crawford going forward.' As it stood, Heineken's takeover of Beamish & Crawford was going to be subject to an investigation either by the Competition Authority in Ireland or by the EU's Competition Commissioner. This was a major commercial deal, and although there was a lot at stake, neither party seemed the type to engage in anything illicit – or so I thought.

I always enjoyed getting a job outside of Dublin, the further away the better, and so when I got the call, I set off for Cork with glee. I had done my research and fully expected a run-of-the-mill TSCM sweep for what looked like a straightforward takeover deal. It would be another night job, but that was okay. I was practically working round the clock these days, anyway: security consultation work by day and commercial counter-espionage by night. I had been contacted through a referral by another consultant and asked to perform a precautionary sweep of their offices prior to the negotiations commencing. The takeover bid by Heineken was by now public knowledge, and I had researched it well. While I expected no foul play by either side, you just never know in this business.

I pulled up to the gates of the brewery and was granted access. After parking the van outside the main offices, I unloaded my kit. I did everything without a thought; commercial counter-espionage was second nature to me now. I had already been given a list of rooms to sweep.

As I did my preliminary walk around, everything looked sweet, until I got to the largest of the offices to be swept. It was there I found the large pile of file boxes. There was no way I could carry out a full physical search of all of them in the time frame I had been given. The military had taught me to improvise, overcome and adapt to any situation – in other words, to stop moaning and get the fucking job done – so I formed a plan. The rest of the rooms would get the full works, a full fingertip search followed by the normal electronic sweep. The main office, however, would be subject to the most intense of electronic sweeps. It would be time-consuming, but to be honest I wasn't expecting any hits that night anyway.

Having finished with all the ancillary rooms, none of which giving any indication of illicit eavesdropping devices, it was now time for the main office. I started with the large NLJD detector and swept the pile of boxes. There was nothing on the first or second sweep. That wasn't enough, though. The height and depth of the boxes would not necessarily give me a return hit. A device could be buried right at the bottom of the pile. It was now time to use the more sensitive handheld detector. I had to get as close as possible to the boxes. This involved clambering over as many of them as I could, careful not to damage or topple the bloody things over. The further I went into the pile of boxes the more the alarm screeched from the detector. There was definitely something wrong here. Paper or cardboard should not set the detector off and certainly not with as such a strong signal as this. Time was running out, so I decided to skip the rest of the handheld search and get the spectrum analyser out. I placed four transmitter/receivers around the pile of boxes, double what I would normally use, set my iPod to play and waited. It was only five minutes into the sweep when I heard the music coming through my headset. Result! I left it playing as I made my way back into the main office, adrenaline now pumping through my body. I switched off one of the transmitter/ receivers and returned to the spectrum analyser to see if the signal was still as strong – it was. I did the same with two more until I had a rough idea where the signal was coming from. Even given the fact that I had narrowed the location down somewhat, it would still be a gargantuan task to find the device in the time frame allowed to me. I sat back at the desk and put the headphones on for one last listen, but the signal was gone, dead! Someone had switched the device off. It could have been coincidence that it had gone off during my sweep, but I didn't believe in coincidences, not in this game. This was why I loved my job: it always threw up more questions than answers. It was time to leave.

After a few hours' sleep in a nearby hotel, I placed a call to my contact. The reaction was somewhat muted, and not what I was expecting at all. None of the usual questions were asked: where did you find it? Are you sure it's a viable bug? Who might have planted it and how? What do we do about it? The main concern seemed to be about how I had found it. I agreed to meet him on-site that night and take him through the operation and location of the device. He was there when I arrived and I walked him straight to the main office. I indicated towards the pile of boxes, but he seemed disinterested and we moved to the car park.

'In answer to your question, it would take someone with the right equipment to find that device. None of your off-the-shelf, spy-shop gear will find it. It was difficult enough for me to find it, and my gear costs a small fortune.

It would also take someone with the right training and background, too. No run-of-the-mill job, this one.'

He was getting his money's worth here and I was letting him know. 'One other thing: the device was switched off at one point, as if someone was live-monitoring it. Was there anyone in the plant that shouldn't have been last night?' I probed.

He didn't answer but posed a question of his own. 'How long do you normally get to do a TSCM sweep before a meeting takes place?'

I thought he was asking so as to bring me in before any proposed meeting with Heineken. 'Depends. For a straightforward meeting, I get about twelve hours beforehand to fully sweep a room.'

He nodded, deep in thought now, but I wanted this one done and dusted, so I started giving him options.

'If you want this extracted I can tear these boxes apart and have it out in a day or so, but it won't be pretty and it will tip your hand.' He was still miles away, but I pressed on. 'I could fit a covert camera and record who comes to retrieve it.'

In a split second, his head whipped round. 'No, that won't be necessary. What would you normally do?'

I rattled off about using the device to feed disinformation to whoever had planted it, but he seemed disinterested in this. I then suggested about live-monitoring and jamming the device. In-Conference Monitoring TSCM or live-monitoring can be provided either overtly via IPMS (In-Place Monitoring System), where I would sit in on any meeting and have my kit operating in full view of those in attendance (a great deterrent but not the most subtle method), or covertly from an adjacent room. This includes monitoring of the radio frequency spectrum (RF

Mapping) to detect any audio, optical or GSM cellular-based technical surveillance threats. It is quick and easy to set up, and will usually rule out any illicit eavesdropping. I had his full attention again.

'Would many companies employ that method? What about jamming – is that often done?' He seemed concerned now.

'It's not that common a practice, but I have known it to be done,' I replied. Then something occurred to me. 'When were these files delivered?' I asked.

'Oh, they weren't delivered. They are our files for due diligence. They'll be looked over by the other side.'

Shit me! Was this a TSCM sweep at all? Or was this to check if I could find a device planted in the files? Were they just checking to see if another TSCM team could find it? Screw this! It was time to smoke this guy out. What if he was using me as a back-door way of planting a device? Fuck that! I was no one's pawn. The time had come to put the frighteners up this guy.

'Well, just as well you hired me, then. I can jam this device anyway, now that I know the frequency it's on. Whoever planted this will probably be using their own ex-military guys, so I'm surprised they advised to plant this in the first place.'

He was now red-faced, and his smile was long gone. Had he been straight with me from the start, I would have told him how to do it properly, maybe. 'So, what's the next step?' I wanted paid and gone out of this job.

'We'll leave it as it is. I'll get some of my guys to search through all the boxes and find it.'

Bollox he would! He knew that I knew. He was caught red-handed, but he was still trying to bluff it out. I had done what I had been asked to do and in this business you learn to walk away and not give it a second thought. You'd be driven crazy otherwise.

It was a few months later that I read the following in a newspaper article: 'Ireland's oldest brewery changed into Dutch hands last night, as Heineken bought out Beamish & Crawford.' The Competition Authority confirmed that it had sanctioned the takeover. Heineken already had a base in Cork but said that it would continue to market the two stouts: its own stout, Murphy's, along with Beamish. However, the merger would lead to the closure of the Beamish & Crawford brewery. Heineken would run all its operation from Leitrim Street in Cork, while Beamish's historic site would cease operations. I didn't know how the other consultant proceeded after I found the device. I wasn't quite sure what had been behind the whole episode. In my professional opinion, it was a very amateur attempt at commercial espionage, one that should have been thrown in the bin. It often occurred to me how much business I could generate if I actually crossed the line and went into commercial espionage. I'd be retired by now. Certainly, in this case, it wasn't all about the beer, more about the money!

Chapter 16

Snow Storm

I gently opened the door of the female toilets and eased my way through. I knocked on each of the cubicles, ensuring that none were occupied. It was highly unlikely that anyone was in the building at this hour, but it was always a case of belt and braces with me. Not a murmur. All clear. The yellow 'Cleaning in Progress' sign that I had placed outside the door should keep anyone else needing to spend a penny at bay while I was working. In the unlikely event that it didn't, the coveralls I was wearing and the kit I was carrying made me look like just another member of the late-night cleaning crew. The usual cleaners weren't due in for another few hours yet, and I had something important to carry out before they could sanitise the building.

The simple and reliable cocaine identification wipes could recognise cocaine residue from minimal amounts of traces present on any surfaces that have been touched by the drug. With the compact size of 2.5 × 3 inches when in the pouch, the wipes provided immediate results with a one-step procedure, while still remaining discreet enough to carry around with me. I removed the wipe from the wrapper and wiped the suspected surface, in this case the bathroom counter tops and tops of the toilet cisterns. If cocaine (or crack/freebase or PCP) was present, the wipe would indicate blue. And there it was! The first swipe indicated blue – cocaine was present – as did the second and all the other surfaces tested in both the male and female toilets on that floor. The wipes were a screening test for information purposes only. Any preliminary positive results would have been confirmed by an alternative methodology before any legal or disciplinary action could be taken. These wipes were a very simple but effective drug-testing kit to use.

I moved from floor to floor, testing all the male and female toilets as I went. Without exception, each of the tested surfaces came back positive for traces of cocaine. I'm not sure what kind of result the client was hoping for, but I doubt that the company I was now working for, the largest professional services firm in Ireland, was expecting this.

The company in question was one of Ireland's largest accountancy firms, taking its share of the almost €1 billion professional services industry during the Celtic Tiger era. Its audit clients include many of Ireland's biggest corporate names spanning all sectors. They audited many of the banks in the years prior to the financial crisis, earning hundreds of millions in fees during the years from 2000 to 2009, the good times! The company also had many State and Semi-State clients and earned millions in fees from advising various government bodies both before and after the banking crisis.

Experts in the fields of assurance, tax, human resources, transactions, performance improvement and crisis management, they were a major global force with a reputation to match and, more importantly, to maintain, hence our visit that night.

I wasn't the main contractor that night. I was sub-contracting to another consultancy firm, but my rate was the same, and, with a little mark-up, it would be passed on to the client. There are lots of reasons why companies carry out testing for drug use in the workplace, most of them valid. Workplace safety is one: all employees have the right to work in a safe environment. It is a legal requirement for each company to have a health and safety policy, of which a drug and alcohol policy should be included. This policy helps reduce the risk of accidents and manage the consequences. Being under the influence of drugs or alcohol in the workplace impairs the ability of an individual to carry out their duties. This is not limited to individuals in charge of heavy or dangerous machinery; those making complex decisions also pose a threat if under the influence. Even if substances are not taken whilst at work, effects from consuming drugs or alcohol outside working hours can last well into the following day. The benefits a company enjoys from having a well-defined drug and alcohol policy enforced by screening programmes include, a lower rate of health insurance, lower levels of absenteeism, and, perhaps, a more productive and collaborative workplace.

None of this really mattered to me. All I knew was I was getting paid for a relatively easy operation. At this stage, the Celtic Tiger had well and truly stopped roaring and I was glad of the money. Things weren't going well with the business. The amount of unpaid invoices owed to me by my clients was ever increasing, as were my bills.

So, what is cocaine and who was using it during the period of the Celtic Tiger and beyond? Cocaine hydrochloride, coke, Charlie or snow, is a stimulant derived from the leaves of the coca bush, which primarily grows in Columbia, Peru and Bolivia. In Ireland, it's available in two forms: cocaine powder (hydrochloride salt) and crack (freebase). The powder is normally snorted, but it can also be turned into liquid form and injected. It's illegal to produce, possess or supply the drug in Ireland, except on prescription, and it's illegal to allow premises to be used for production or supply.

One could now understand why a company with a global reputation didn't want anyone using the drug on their premises. The effects of taking cocaine start quickly and last for around thirty minutes. These effects include a sense of euphoria, heightened alertness, impaired judgement and a delusional and overblown view of one's self-importance. After extended use, users need to take larger doses to feel the same high. Cocaine users can become unpredictable. Combining cocaine with alcohol is particularly risky, as when taken together the two join forces to produce another drug – cocaethylene. This is more toxic than using coke or alcohol on its own. Users often report a dry mouth, a loss of appetite and an increased heart rate. Cocaine use can cause headaches, stomach pains, nausea, tremors, paranoia and hallucinations, but alarmingly, it leads to a thickening of the blood which can subsequently lead to strokes and seizures. Heart attacks are the most common cause of death for coke users. If heavy users stop using cocaine they often encounter a 'crash', which can involve restlessness, tiredness and depression. In the early days, it was seen as a 'high-end' drug taken by the very wealthy, but it quickly made its way into mainstream use as the country enjoyed the boom times. During the Celtic Tiger, between 2000 and 2005, cocaine use increased by as much as 800%. Ireland was ranked as third in Europe for cocaine use. The Tallaght Cocaine Pilot Study in the mid-1990s showed that heavy binge users in the South Dublin district were spending between €200 and €2,000 over a three- or four-day weekend. In post-Tiger Ireland, however, the price of half a gram of coke dropped to €20 as a result of a fall in demand and the flooding of the market (half the price you'd have paid back in the boom days). It means that a line of coke now costs less than a pint of beer in a pub.

Coke became a fashionable drug, as common as alcohol in many circles, and some of Ireland's most high-profile figures were caught up in it. In certain social circles, it almost became acceptable. Broadcaster Gerry Ryan and the model and socialite Katy French were among those who were suspected to have died from cocaine-related use. It was claimed by many of the Irish newspapers at the time of his death that Ryan occasionally took cocaine while at work in RTÉ in order to help him get through his three-hour radio show every day. *The Irish Mail on Sunday* claimed that the DJ was known by many in RTÉ to have been a regular cocaine user, though the star had tried to mask it with champagne and Valium. It also quoted a former colleague of Ryan, 4FM broadcaster Gareth O'Callaghan, who claimed that his cocaine use was 'widely known in both RTÉ Radio 1 and 2FM'. The star would apparently pay 'over the odds' for the volume of the drug he would use, it claims, in order to keep his habit a secret. Confirmation of Ryan's cocaine use came when an inquest into his death found traces of the drug in his bloodstream and returned a verdict of death by misadventure. Back in 2007, 24-year-old Katy French died after taking cocaine at an event to celebrate her birthday. So now the young and trendy professionals of Ireland, with their seemingly unending disposable income, would follow the example of Ireland's celebrities, and nowhere was that more evident than at the offices of the company I was working in that night.

Of course, the tests that were carried out that night were far from conclusive. In order to prove that there was a consistent use of drugs during the working day, we would have to clean the surfaces down and return for a retest. As we cleaned each of the surfaces, we retested with the tester kits to ensure that they all now showed negative for traces of cocaine. I was tempted to add a very strong bleach to the cleaning solution we were using, to give anyone doing a line of coke a very nasty shock, thus delivering my own brand of justice, but I wasn't there for that. We made our exit with a plan to return the following night to carry out the tests once more and file a report for the company.

The contact at this company was informed of our preliminary findings and gave us the go-ahead to do the retest the following night. The procedure was the same, each set of bathroom facilities on every floor was tested in the same manner as the previous night, and all tested positive for traces of cocaine again. Even I was shocked by this. I had assumed that the tests the previous night were an accumulation built up over a period of time, not an everyday occurrence. The scale of the drug use seemed to be at extraordinary levels. My part in this operation was complete. A report would be written and passed on to whoever had commissioned the tests from this large professional services firm. As far as I was concerned, there were grounds for both an internal investigation and a criminal investigation led by the Gardaí. After all, someone was supplying all this cocaine. As far as I know, neither ever happened. It seemed the use of drugs, in particular cocaine, by celebrities and the wealthy was not viewed in the same light as drug use by lower classes. This was made clear by the attendance of the aide-de-camp (ADC) of the then Taoiseach, Bertie Aherne, at the funeral of Katy French. French, just like those using cocaine at many high-profile companies, was breaking the law. Her use of cocaine was illegal and fuelled a violent, gangland struggle for the lucrative drug market. No ADC was sent to the funerals of the approximately 600 other drug-related deaths that year – it seemed they didn't fit the right profile to warrant the government's sympathy.

In 2015, many professional services companies were called before the Oireachtas Banking Inquiry, as they had been the auditors for many of the country's financial institutions. Most of these companies claimed that changes had been made in how they operated since the crisis. The millions of euros in fees that had been paid to many of these companies was raised. The inquiry was told that it was not the role of these companies to give an opinion on any institution's business model, and they denied they were complacent despite giving the banks a clean bill of health months before the crisis.

Given the vital role that the company I had carried out the drug test for, and other firms, play in the auditing of Irish financial institutions, and given what I had learned about the conduct of some of their employees, a fair question to ask is: who is watching the watchers?

Chapter 17

The Walls Have Ears

By now I had been in every prison in the country, including the Dóchas Centre (Ireland's female-only prison), but I still couldn't get used to the heavy doors slamming behind us as the prison guard escorted us from the main gate. On this occasion, my colleague Phil and I were entering Wheatfield prison in Clondalkin. Everything we had was handed in at the security control point before we walked through the metal detectors, and we were given a pat-down by the prison search teams. All we had left on us were our notebooks and pens, but that was all we would need today. It wasn't my first time in Wheatfield prison and it wouldn't be my last. Neither Phil nor I were inmates, of course, we were there as observers.

The constant jangling of the guards' keys always unnerved me. I don't know why, but it felt like I was no longer in control of where I went, or when. I guess in truth I wasn't; it was down to our prison escort. The guards took us to the prison control room, where our interest lay that day. We were viewed with some suspicion by the prison officers at every prison we visited, but we were really there to help them, to try to make their jobs easier and safer. Sometimes it takes time to convince people of that. I didn't envy the prison officers. They were hugely undermanned and the technology they had to work with was, in my view, archaic.

We took our seats at the rear of the control room, sitting behind the two duty officers, and we all stared at the bank of CCTV monitors and remote-access control panels for the various doors and gates around the prison blocks. As each request came through from the prison officers on the landings for the gates to be opened, the officers in the control room had to get up and lean across the control panel in order to hit the release button for that gate. It doesn't sound too bad, does it? Until you have to do it twenty times a minute. Even from our position I could see that the images from the video cameras were terrible. You couldn't really tell who was who from some of the images. I also knew that this wasn't how things normally operated here. If we weren't there, things would definitely have been different in this control room. It was time to find out how different.

'Look, we are not here to judge how you do things, but we can only help improve prison operations if we know how bad things really are. None of what we see here today will go beyond me and the rest of the design team,' I assured the female prison officer sitting at the control desk.

She wasn't totally convinced but looked at her colleague with a raised eyebrow. He nodded and she pulled a short-shaft pool cue from beneath the desk. As each request for gates to be opened came from the landings, she no longer got up to see who was on the camera or to push the release button; she simply used the pool cue to push the button from the comfort of her seat. This is what we needed to see: how the prison really operated on a day-today basis. It would provide us with the basis for the design of Ireland's first super-prison – Thornton Hall.

The site for Thornton Hall, a 150-acre greenfield plot at Kilsallaghan near Swords, north Dublin, was bought in controversial circumstances for €30 million in 2005 to replace Mountjoy Prison, which inspectors had branded unacceptable and unfit for inmates. The price per acre was far higher than any other land sales in the area at that time, almost double. It was planned that the new prison would house 1,400 inmates if prisoners were kept one to a cell. The design would have the capacity to hold more than one prisoner in most cells, giving a 2,200 maximum occupancy. This would be no ordinary prison. It would be ten individual prisons in one – a campus-style prison. Each of the ten prisons would have its own individual security system, including anti-climb outer walls, high-security gates, search facilities, CCTV and access control systems, but it would also be surrounded by one shared external wall, a gate and search system, CCTV and access control equipment. Everything was to be controlled from each individual prison, but the main control room for the campus could take over at any point, should any of the prisons become compromised. It would be a state-of-the-art facility in every aspect. It was hoped the design of the prison would remove the problem of illegal contraband, such as drugs, mobile phones and weapons, from entering the prison system. For some within the design team, myself included, the new prison went too far with regard to prisoner comforts. Each cell would be en-suite, with a TV with more channels than I had at home. The planned recreation, gym and educational facilities would put any university or college in Ireland to shame. It didn't live up to my idea of a prison. The best design for a prison that

I had ever seen was in Freetown, Sierra Leone, during the civil war there. It consisted of four walls, four guard towers complete with machine-gun nests and a lean-to. If you approached the wall you were shot without warning, and the lean-to was the only shelter provided from the elements. A diet of rice and water was the prisoners' only food, if relatives didn't deliver food to the gates every day. Now that's a deterrent! Spending your days in the luxury of the proposed Thornton Hall wasn't, at least in my opinion.

I was part of the security design team with Léargas, a consortium led by Bernard McNamara, who was one of Ireland's most successful property developers. Léargas had been chosen as the preferred bidder to design and construct the new Thornton Hall prison complex as a public–private partnership (PPP) with the State.

The consortium was comprised of Michael McNamara Construction, Barclays Private Equity and GSL, a prisons' operator. HKR Architects, a Dublin-based firm, had been contracted to design the new prison. It was initially thought the project would cost about €400 million. Under the terms of the PPP, Léargas would pay for the costs of the design and construction up front. It would then receive fixed payments from the State over a 25-year period. The consortium would also be responsible for the provision of certain services at the prison. It was a very lucrative contract. Construction was due to begin by 2008, with Thornton Hall scheduled to open before the end of 2010. There wasn't a chance in hell of that happening. The Thornton Hall project was already mired in controversy: local residents had objected to its construction, citing poor road access to the site. The government had also suggested relocating the central mental hospital in Dundrum to Thornton Hall.

Prison designs are far from straightforward, and Thornton Hall would be trickier than most. Not only were the cells to be tested to destruction, and I mean to destruction, but there was a further requirement that was very unusual and completely off the books. It had first been raised during testing by Léargas at the Glass Bottle site in Dublin's Docklands.

Back in 2006, when land in Ballsbridge was more expensive than Paris, this site was seen as the single best development opportunity in the country. Bought by a consortium led by Bernard McNamara and including Derek Quinlan and the Dublin Docklands Development Authority (DDDA), the 24-acre site had, in 2006, major potential. The fast-track planning of the DDDA was a key component of the development scheme. It was, unsurprisingly, Anglo Irish Bank who backed the deal with a €288 million loan. DDDA chairman Lar Bradshaw sat on the Anglo board, and Anglo chairman Seán FitzPatrick sat on the DDDA board – all very cosy indeed. With expected clean-up and construction costs of €3,300 per square metre and expected sales of almost €8,000 per square metre, this seemed like a no-brainer for McNamara.

It was McNamara's involvement in the Glass Bottle site that allowed Léargas to carry out our tests on various cell designs we were proposing for Thornton Hall there. On the day in question, we had one of the proposed pod-design cells at the site. Members of the Irish Prison Service (IPS) were there to test the cell for potential design flaws. In reality, this meant they wanted to see if they could take the cell apart, and, to be honest, they did so with ease. Several security flaws were identified, but that was all part of the process. Among the IPS personnel were some of the negotiating team. As I stood there taking notes on the destruction that had just been inflicted on one of our proposed pods, one of the senior IPS negotiators sidled up to me. He wanted to talk about the vandal-proof intercoms that we were proposing to install in the prison cells. Made by Zenitel, the intercoms were state-of-the-art, IP-based systems which allowed for two-way voice operation.

'The microphone on the intercom, can it be activated remotely?' he enquired.

'Of course. Anyone back at the control room can switch it on,' I answered, without thinking.

But that wasn't what he was asking. He clarified by saying, 'No, I mean can it be activated without the prisoner knowing it's on?'

Now I fully understood what he meant. He wanted to know if the microphone that formed part of the intercom could be used as a covert listening device to listen in on prisoners' conversations. This was interesting. None of this had been mentioned in the specification that had been put forward by the IPS in the tender process, nor had it been mentioned at any of our previous design meetings with the IPS. I knew full well that the system could easily carry out the task that they wanted, but I needed to go back and discuss this with the others on the team before confirming.

Noting the pause in my response, he added, 'This is something we would very much like to keep between ourselves. Just between the security design team and the OSG guys.'

I indicated that there would be no problem and I would get back to him. OSG (Operational Support Group) and OSU (Operational Support Unit) were the IPS teams that carried out searches and gathered intelligence within the prison system. They were also an integral part of the negotiating team; they knew every trick the prisoners might use to beat the new proposed prison.

I raised the matter with the rest of the team the following day at our usual design meeting. No one seemed to have an issue with it, but I wondered just how legal it was to listen into prisoners' private conversations in their cells. To be honest, I just didn't know if it was legal or not. It wasn't the only unusual aspect of the negotiating process with the IPS. Members of the Léargas security design team were using a contact, a retired prison governor, to get the inside track on what the minimum level of security measures the IPS negotiators would accept. We knew their back-stop position before each meeting, a real advantage in the negotiations. I decided to test how legitimate the request for covert eavesdropping on the cells really was. At the next meeting at the IPS offices near the Red Cow roundabout in Dublin, I raised the issue.

We were all sitting around the table, the Léargas team on one side and the IPS team on the other. Before the meeting started, as innocently as possible, I called across the desk to the former prison governor who spoke to me a few days previously about the Zenitel intercoms.

'I checked that out for you, and, yes, the microphone can be turned on remotely without the prisoner ever knowing you are listening in.'

The look that was shot across the desk at me was nearly as hostile as the boot underneath the table from the head of the design team sitting beside me. So, they really didn't want it brought up in meetings. I left it at that and no more was said, at least not until we took a coffee break. In the ground-floor canteen, I was cornered by two of the IPS team.

'We want that kept quiet. That is never to be mentioned in a meeting again. It will only ever be discussed on the sidelines.'

I saw two possibilities here: firstly, everything was above board and they just wanted the capability as an ace up their sleeves to enhance their intelligence-gathering capabilities or, secondly, what they were proposing was legally questionable. It would never amount to anything anyway.

The PPP scheme between Léargas and the Irish government for the building and running of Thornton Hall was everything that was wrong with the Celtic Tiger. Huge amounts of money were spent on overpriced land and costs spiralled out of control. The cost of the project had increased by at least 25%, mainly due to additional requests from the IPS and the additional cost of financing the project. The wining and dining of the decision makers, in this case the IPS, by suppliers seemed endless. I remember one trip in particular to Sheffield. The entire design team, including the IPS team, was taken across to the UK to view the proposed control system for the electronic security systems. No expense was spared on food, drink and hotels. Ultimately, it would not matter. The collapse of the Irish financial system would put an end to Thornton Hall.

It happened so suddenly. We all showed up to attend a meeting at one of McNamara's offices in Dublin one morning, only to find the doors shut and the project over. The government would reveal that it could not afford to press ahead with plans for the massive prison complex in north Dublin. Almost €11 million had already been spent on consultants' fees for the scheme, which was to solve the serious overcrowding conditions in Mountjoy. The

IPS had broken off long-running negotiations with the Léargas Consortium, leaving many of us sub-contractors with huge unpaid bills. The then justice minister, Dermot Ahern, who had warned that major state projects could be hit by the recession, said a new, cheaper project was needed.

'What is now needed is a new project which reflects the current economic and fiscal realities and protects the taxpayers' interests,' he said.

IPS officials and advisers said the project was unaffordable at the price quoted by Léargas and based on the increased cost of lending. 'In the current economic circumstances a more affordable solution for the Exchequer is required,' an IPS spokesman said.

In 2015, the Thornton Hall site was valued at just €2.4 million, a fraction of the price paid for it in 2006. It had become Ireland's most expensive field, used by inmates from other prisons in Dublin to grow vegetables.

Regardless, should I ever find myself incarcerated in an Irish prison, I'll be careful what I say. After all, the walls may have ears!

Chapter 18

A Not-So-Private Collection

As predicted, the security light came on and bathed the courtyard in a soft glow. I and anyone else that might have been around ignored it. Animals of all shapes and sizes set the sensors off all the time, making them more of a nuisance than anything else. Besides, it was two in the morning, and I was sticking to the shadows as I made my way towards the side of the building. My dark clothing and hooded jacket kept me hidden from the outdated security cameras covering the courtyard. I made my way to the small window that stood about chest high. I peered through and spotted the magnetic sensor that was attached to the window. The first job of the night was to defeat that without setting off the intruder alarm. Most window alarms work via a magnet. There is a sensor on the inside of the window frame that is wired up to the security system. Then there is a magnet attached to the window. If the magnet moves away from the sensor, the circuit is broken and the alarm sounds. Using a screwdriver, I gently eased the window open, sliding a small flat fridge magnet in place as I did so. The fridge magnet would keep the circuit intact and prevent the alarm from going off. With the magnet in place, I was free to open the window fully. I didn't enter the building, though, not yet. I removed the powerful infrared beam from my pocket, switched it on and pointed it towards the PIR sensor mounted on the ceiling. The intruder alarm sounded instantly. I switched the beam off, closed the window, slowly removing the fridge magnet as I did so, thus keeping the circuit intact. I made my way back across the courtyard, the bell ringing in my ears. Stage one was successfully completed.

The directions I had been given took me deep into the west of Ireland, not to the country manor house I was expecting, but to a large farmhouse, owned by my very wealthy client. The farmhouse was just one of many properties he owned in the area. Every time a property or piece of land came up for sale near or adjacent to it, he bought it. He didn't rent out the properties or anything; he just didn't want strangers around him. Some of the properties had been left idle for years, but others he had converted into galleries for his enormous art collection. Many of the old outbuildings had been lovingly restored and now housed priceless works of art. It was his wife who greeted me at the door and led me to the kitchen where I found her husband, complete with wellington boots, poring over the local newspaper with a mug of tea in hand. He was straight to the point.

'I want you to evaluate the security system for me. Let me know if it needs upgrading,' he grunted, without looking up.

I could have told him from first glance that it did indeed need upgrading, but I thought of a better plan. 'I can try to break in if you like? Steal something.'

His head whipped up from the newspaper and his weathered face broke into a smile. 'I like the sound of that.'

He offered to walk me around the buildings containing his art collection but I declined. 'That would give me an unfair advantage. You wouldn't walk any other would-be thief through your premises, would you?' I asked.

His smile got even broader. He liked my honesty. A fair contest. The premises was covered by a basic CCTV and intruder alarm system, more suitable for a domestic house than a private art collection. The system had been supplied and installed by a local security company that also provided the house and surrounding buildings with routine patrols and an alarm response service.

'No tipping the security company off that I'm coming, now,' I laughed.

'No chance,' he assured me.

I left and made the long drive back to Dublin, after promising I'd make an attempt in the coming weeks.

Work in security design had dried up and I was surviving on the few TSCM sweeps and jobs like this I was getting. The fucking banks had screwed us all! So, I had plenty of time to plan the upcoming burglary. I had spent years teaching others how to bypass security systems. Back then it was known as CMOE – Covert Methods Of Entry – and it was something of an art form. I had little doubt that I could lift something from the premises without anyone even noticing. It would start on the following Thursday night and before the weekend was over I would have a piece of the client's collection in my hands. Best of all, neither the security company nor the client would be any the wiser.

I parked my 4x4 in a small lay-by about a mile from the house. No rental car this time – funds were tight. I had everything I would need to stay on the grounds for a week if necessary, including all the items crucial for a CMOE.

The key to any surveillance operation, and in particular, a covert break-in, is patience and attention to detail. I made my way from the parked vehicle to a spot overlooking the main house and outbuildings where I knew much of the art collection was stored. I set up my OP (Observation Post) below the treeline on the crest of the hill, ensuring that it wasn't silhouetted against the skyline. In another life, not too long ago, all this would have been done in camouflage gear and a sniper suit; a proper hide would have been built and I would have remained in position for the duration of the operation. There was no need for such dramatics on this job; besides, being found by a Garda patrol in a sniper suit in rural west of Ireland might have taken some explaining. I settled in for the night, taking out a pack of my favourite Biltong, South African dried meat, to keep my concentration levels up. My tools for tonight were my notepad and pen, binoculars, screwdriver, fridge magnet and my infrared beam – nothing else was needed.

The mobile patrol from the security company did its first sweep of the premises at nine o'clock that night. The security guard never even left the comfort of his patrol vehicle. A cursory glance to ensure no windows were broken and that no unauthorised vehicles were around was sufficient for this guy. I noted the time and how long he stayed. Each patrol was fairly predictable: it would arrive about every two hours and spend a total of ten minutes on-site.

It was getting warm, and I was starting to sweat beneath my layers of clothing, so I welcomed the cooling breeze when I finally got up to approach the property to set off the alarm. I had chosen the converted barn furthest from the main house as my target. The security equipment there looked the oldest, as if it had been reused from another building. I was tempted to just force the front door and try the last digits of the security firm telephone number that were displayed on the alarm bell box, to disarm the system. Believe it or not, that often works. Because the turn-around of security engineers is usually quite high, rather than changing the universal engineering code for the alarms every time an engineer leaves, they simply use the last digits of the company's phone number. With the alarm now blaring across the countryside I made my way back to my OP and waited. It took just short of fifteen minutes for the patrol to return – not bad. This time the security guard got out of the vehicle and walked around the building, checking doors and windows as he went along. I watched through my binoculars as he eventually used the remote key fob to switch the alarm off. No lights had come on in the main farmhouse. I wasn't sure if the client was away or was just playing the game by ignoring the alarm and leaving it to the alarm company.

Twice more I returned to the converted barn that night and activated the alarm in exactly the same manner. Each time the security patrol returned, I noted its response times were slower. On the third occasion, a security technician arrived after the security patrol. I watched with interest as he entered the building, but I knew what he would do. He would discover on logging into the system that the PIR that I had hit with the infrared beam was the sensor setting the alarm off. Given that they now would have confirmed that no one had entered the building, he would replace the sensor. Of course what they should have done was to check the CCTV footage to see if anyone had been around the premises when the alarm was triggered, but I knew that wouldn't happen because that would take time and both were now coming towards the end of their shifts. It would simply be put down to a faulty sensor – exactly what I wanted, for now. The temptation would have been to let the patrol leave and make my entry there and then, but I had learned the long game. Besides, I was thoroughly enjoying myself.

I returned again on the Friday night and carried out the same procedure. By now the patrol company was sick to the back teeth of the alarm going off and I could only imagine the bollocking the duty alarm engineer was getting. He was back again now to try and find the phantom fault. It was obvious what the conclusion would be: a line or wiring fault. So the sensor would be isolated completely until they could come back on Monday morning with a full crew and rerun the wiring for the PIR sensor. I watched as they left. I didn't set the alarm off again that night. I wanted to build their confidence in their belief that they had successfully found the fault. They wouldn't be too concerned. The doors and windows all had fully working sensors on them, or so they thought. Happy with my night's work, I left and headed for a local hotel for a shower and a few hours' sleep. Saturday night would be the final night for this one.

This time I watched the mobile patrol leave from my car. There was no need for an OP now. As it drove away, I eased the car down the road, lights off, and stopped a few hundred metres from the target building. I didn't want to have to move too far on foot with a painting in hand. The quicker I could get it into the back of the vehicle and covered, the better. I gave it ten minutes, which would leave me just over an hour before the patrol would return again – plenty of time. I walked straight across the courtyard this time, brazen as you like; the sensor lights and CCTV didn't bother me now. The best way to defeat a CCTV system is to wear a hood – if they can't see your face, they can't prove it's you. I opened the side window once more, careful to keep the circuit intact using the fridge magnet. I was confident that the PIR sensor had been isolated, but I still held my breath as I lowered myself through the window and into the gallery. I took two steps. No alarm sounded. It was time to pick something to steal. I wasn't here to make a dramatic statement, just to show that I could gain entry, lift something and leave without anyone knowing. I spotted a small painting, about two foot square, and decided that I would have that one. I first checked behind the painting to make sure there were no security contacts on the back that would sound if I removed the painting. There were none. I carefully removed the painting and laid it on the floor. Next, I removed a roll of bubble wrap from under my hoodie. This thing was going to be wrapped up like the baby Jesus. I had no idea how much it was worth and the thought of footing the bill if I damaged it made me more than a little nervous. Once wrapped up it was time to go. It was as easy leaving as it was getting in. I quickly made my way back to the car and checked my watch. I had thirty minutes to spare. I carefully secured the painting into the boot of my car and covered it with a blanket. As I drove off towards Dublin and home, I chuckled to myself. I could make a living from this. Breaking into any premises is easy; breaking in and not getting caught is good; breaking in without anyone even realising, now, that is a work of art!

It was Sunday evening when the call came through.

'I seriously hope that it's you who has it,' the voice on the other end said.

I had a smile from ear-to-ear as I answered. 'Yes, I've got it. Just out of curiosity, is it worth much?'

He was now the one laughing as he replied, 'No, only a few thousand euros. You missed all the really valuable ones. You could have cleaned me out, you bastard. How did you do it? The alarm company said there was a faulty sensor, but I guess that was you?'

I simply laughed and told him that I couldn't give away the trade secrets. My little experiment had caused huge embarrassment to the security company. I was now tasked with designing a new security system – cost was not an issue – and to draw up new operating procedures for the mobile patrols in the event of an alarm going off. I'm often asked what the best security system is, and my answer is always the same: while electronic security systems are useful, they should only be used as an enhancement for strong physical security. Good locks on your doors and windows, along with a dog, will serve you much better than an electronic security system on its own. With patience, anything can be achieved and there is no such thing as a private collection or an impregnable premises, at least not while the likes of me are around!

Chapter 19

A Different Type of Tiger

'Your wife and children are being held at a secret location. Be under no illusion, if the money isn't transferred within the hour, they will come to a very violent end. All you have to do is go into your office, log into the system and transfer the money to the account number you have been given. If you fail to do so or alert the authorities in any way, your family will be killed. Are you prepared to take that risk? Can you put a price on your family's lives?'

The almost bored look that only a few minutes before had been on the executive's face was now replaced by the grim realisation that I wasn't joking. This could all be very real. Tiger kidnappings in Ireland were on the increase, and gangs were prepared to kill for far smaller sums of money than this gentleman could put his hands on. We had just exposed a major flaw in the financial security of one of Ireland's biggest commercially run Semi-State bodies, EirGrid.

In July 2006, after a five-year delay, the national grid system became the responsibility of a new state-owned company called EirGrid, rather than the ESB. A statutory instrument was introduced in 2001 on the back of an EU directive to set up EirGrid as a separate entity from the ESB. But wrangling had been going on since then about transferring ESB staff to the new body. Private sector electricity companies had been calling for the establishment of the new company for several years, but various attempts to address staff concerns failed, causing the delays in setting the new company up. The company would have its own board of directors and a commercial mandate. It would act as the transmission system operator for Ireland. While the new company would have no links to the ESB, the national grid assets would remain in the ownership of the ESB. The national grid is made up of more than 5,800 km of high voltage lines and cables, the majority of which would now be controlled by EirGrid.

EirGrid was to be run by managing director Dermot Byrne. Byrne was an electrical engineer and had extensive senior management experience in the electricity industry, mostly with the ESB. He was appointed Chief Executive of EirGrid in July 2005. Byrne was a graduate of University College Dublin and held a Master's in both Electrical Engineering and Business Administration. He also qualified as a Chartered Director from the Institute of Directors. He was one of the main reasons Phil and I had been hired by the EirGrid's national security manager. Our task was two-fold: first, to carry out an evaluation of Byrne's personal security, and second to evaluate the security of EirGrid as a whole.

Byrne's home was what you would expect of the CEO of a major company: plush and in the right area of Dublin, the wealthy area with its tree-lined avenues and pretty parks. I arrived at his home on a Saturday morning. He was there himself to let me in and show me around. A nice enough fellow, he let me get on with what I needed to do after the obligatory offer of coffee, which I politely refused.

I questioned him on some of the aspects of his security and his routine and made the appropriate notes. All this would form part of the briefing we would later give him and the written report that would follow.

But Dermot Byrne's personal security wasn't the main problem we found, hence the reason we were briefing him on so-called tiger kidnappings. While running through the company list to see who had access to what information, we identified that this man, on his own, could electronically access the financial accounts of EirGrid. With that capability came the option of transferring money from the accounts without the need for a secondary confirmation. This was solid gold for any would-be tiger kidnapper. We were talking millions of euros here. There would be no need for large amounts of cash to be hauled about the place, just a few keystrokes and millions could be wired to the account of your choice. Once there, it would disappear into a dozen other accounts across the world, to be used at the perpetrator's leisure. At first, the guy just didn't get it, but with the description of the tiger kidnapping now permanently etched into his brain, he realised how vulnerable both he and the system really were. Immediate steps were taken to rectify the situation, including the use of distress codes built into the login process. If the distress login was entered into the system, the alarm would be silently raised, while the system would apparently continue to operate as normal. It was the first of many issues that we discovered at EirGrid.

The evaluation of the security of EirGrid's physical locations was our next task. The company's main headquarters was located at the Oval, Shelbourne Road, in Ballsbridge, Dublin. It was here that the main control room for the national grid was housed. Although it was a truly impressive setup, ultra-modern in every way, its security was vulnerable on a number of fronts. The security of the building on initial inspection was good. Electronic access control points to enter the building, CCTV systems and manned security points protected both the building and the control room itself. But none of this was designed to stop a forced entry, and, at this moment in time, a forced entry was a possibility. The proposed EirGrid North-South Interconnector had rallied a number of environmental protest groups to try to prevent it going ahead. The North-South Interconnector would be a new 400 kV overhead line that would connect the electricity grids in Ireland and Northern Ireland. It would require some 400 pylons between Meath and Tyrone. The environmental groups preferred the underground option, but this was viewed as too expensive and was highly unlikely to happen. So a sit-in protest or something similar to prevent staff entering or leaving the building, or even an attempt to gain control of the control room itself, was not to be ruled out. It was the North–South element, however, that had us most concerned. That had prompted a number of subversive dissident republican elements to infiltrate the environmental protest groups. Since the 1970s, the IRA had violently objected to any link between the two power grids, and now with the peace process in place, the dissident movement had taken on the mantle. I needed to know how deeply they had infiltrated the protest groups, so it was time to call in a few favours from my mates across the border. This wasn't a conversation to have over the phone, so I dispatched Phil to Northern Ireland to find out what he could.

The news wasn't good. A number of people I was acquainted with during my time in Northern Ireland were now supporting the protest groups, and I suspected that most of the genuine protestors didn't know about their more militant backgrounds. The subversive element would later become apparent when explosive devices were placed around some pylons in the border counties. These guys meant business and it was time to let EirGrid, in particular its security manager and CEO, know exactly where its vulnerabilities lay. We arranged to give both men a briefing at their offices in Ballsbridge the following week. Both Phil and I had vast experience in delivering briefings, both in the military and in the commercial world. We tended to keep it short and sharp, knowing that those we were briefing were busy and had little interest in details; they had others for that. With both men now seated in a conference room, we began. We worked without notes, covering the main topics, such as personal security, subversion, sabotage, terrorism, cybersecurity, etc. We highlighted, in particular, the vulnerabilities of the control room and its backup site to sit-in or violent protest. We also demonstrated how EirGrid staff could be subject to abuse because they all had a habit of wearing their EirGrid identity tags outside of the workplace, a very stupid thing to do. However, it was obvious to Phil and I that Byrne had no interest in listening to what we had to say. It was time for a wake-up call. I winked at Phil – good cop, bad cop time. I aimed my next question directly at Dermot Byrne.

'I don't want you to tell me, but think of how much money you could put your hands on today, if you really needed to. Be realistic.'

Of course, I had a fair idea of exactly how much money he had and let me tell you it wasn't insignificant.

Then Phil jumped in and in his harshest Belfast accent said, 'I know people who would kill you and your family for half that amount.' Coming from him, it sounded even more ominous.

Finally, we had his attention. It made no difference to either of us if Byrne and his colleagues took on board what we were telling them, but it might make a real difference to him and his family.

He sat up a little straighter in his chair and nodded. 'What are you recommending?'

Everything was in the report that we had given to the national security manager, including all the changes in procedures, additional security measures and personal security assessments. I'm glad to say that EirGrid implemented many of our recommendations. After all, we had just demonstrated that there was more than one type of tiger operating in Ireland.

Chapter 20

Old Foes

My hands were sweating as I gripped the steering wheel, inching the car slowly towards the PSNI VCP (Vehicle Check Point) ahead. I was about four cars away and was tempted to turn and hotfoot it back the way I came as quick as I could, but I doubted I would have gotten very far. They were pulling about every fourth or fifth vehicle over for a random search, but I knew from experience that there was nothing random in Northern Ireland. Somewhere in this line of traffic was a target that the PSNI wanted. I was just hoping I wasn't it. The package in the boot of my car now worried me greatly. I knew it wasn't dangerous as such, but it would take an awful lot of answers to explain it away and I didn't fancy a night in the cells at Strand Road PSNI station. I knew what had gone on there over the years and, even though times had changed since the bad old days of the RUC, I knew you could still disappear here in Northern Ireland.

Back in the old days, a quick call over the radio would have seen me sail through this checkpoint, but I no longer had that luxury. I knew if I was pulled here it was a case of 'on your own, Jack'. No help would come from the people I was working for, whoever they were. It had been a poor decision to try and cross the border at Derry; it was too well policed. I should have pushed on for Strabane or further down to Aughnacloy. But I'd been impatient, keen to cross the border as soon as possible and get the job done. I was next and as I approached the checkpoint I lowered my window, careful to keep my hands clearly visible. I was driving a vehicle registered in the Republic; that alone would attract attention. I was also very conscious of the two other PSNI officers providing cover with their H&K assault rifles. Not too long ago I would have had one in the vehicle myself, with a 9 mm pistol to back it up.

The officer stuck his head in the window. 'Where you heading, sir?'

'Letterkenny and then on to Mayo,' I replied, with as much confidence as I could muster. After what seemed like an eternity, he nodded and waved me through the checkpoint. I obviously wasn't who they were looking for that day, thank fuck.

All favours have to be repaid, and the ones I had called in over the last few years from old colleagues in Northern Ireland while I was working back home would be no different. Coincidentally, the favour I was returning would be linked to an enquiry I had made into subversive activity among environmental groups operating in the Republic. The call had been straightforward: a meet at McDonald's just outside the Waterside area of Derry. Despite the miserable weather, Ted, my old camera technician mate, was sitting outside on one of the benches, milkshake in hand. I sat across from him and he slid a tray of fries in front of me.

'Chip?' he asked, then laughed.

We spent ten minutes talking shite before he finally got down to brass tacks. 'Got a job I need a hand with, mate.

The client needs an asset put in to keep tabs on someone. Unfortunately, it's in your neck of the woods and I really don't feel like crossing the border.'

Ted was Scottish but was shacked up with some bird from Lisburn for the past ten years so was permanently in Northern Ireland now, as far as I knew. I didn't know if Ted was still in the military or not and I wasn't about to ask. The less I knew about his 'client' the better. By 'asset' I knew he was referring to a surveillance asset: either a camera, listening or tracking device, none of which I wanted to be carrying around with me, not on this side of the border. But fair is fair, so I nodded and he slipped a piece of paper across the table. I looked at it and memorised the six-figure grid reference scribbled on it before handing it back.

'Target is a small culvert at the northern edge of the field. Neat and discreet please, mate. This anti-Shell crowd have a few of our old friends involved with them. Just need to know if they have any spectaculars planned,' he added, as he pushed an envelope across the table. 'For your trouble.'

With that he got up and left, leaving a small backpack behind for me – the asset. I gave him ten minutes and, satisfied that he was now clear, I took the backpack and placed it in the boot of the car.

As I made my way across the border towards Letterkenny, I tried to recall what I knew of the Shell-Corrib fiasco. In 1996, the Corrib gas field discovery was declared by Enterprise Energy Ireland Ltd, which submitted plans to pump it ashore and build an onshore refinery in north Mayo. The rights to the Corrib field were acquired by Shell in April 2002, and they became the lead developer with Norwegian company Statoil; Marathon Oil was also involved. As quickly as May 2002, the Minister for the Marine, Frank Fahey, signed a compulsory acquisition order for access to private lands in and around Rossport for the onshore pipeline route required by Shell, but twelve months later, in 2003, An Bord Pleanála refused planning permission for the Ballinaboy onshore terminal. Inspector Kevin Moore described it as the 'wrong site' from a strategic planning, balanced regional development, environment and sustainable-impact perspective. In September 2003, Taoiseach Bertie Ahern stepped in when he and two ministers met the Shell president and senior management in Dublin. Shortly after, a revised application for the gas terminal was submitted by Shell and was approved in October 2004 with forty-two conditions. But the controversy raged on when, in June 2005, the High Court jailed five men who became known as the 'Rossport Five' for contempt of court over their continued protests over the pipeline route. Three months later they would be released when Shell dropped their injunction. The Environmental Protection Agency (EPA) granted an emissions licence for the Ballinaboy terminal in November 2007. By early 2009 things took a turn for the worse when dissident republican elements became involved.

It was claimed in the media that dissident republicans linked to the groups that carried out the murders of two soldiers and a policeman in Northern Ireland in March 2009 were responsible for the break-in and criminal damage of the Shell gas plant in Mayo in April of that year. The group of around eighteen men, wearing black balaclavas, threatened and struck one of the two security guards on duty with an iron bar before causing damage costing thousands of euros in what Garda sources described as a 'military-style' operation. They used bolt cutters to break into the compound before stealing a mechanical digger and destroying fencing and the entrance gates. A delivery lorry was also heavily vandalised, and when additional security staff arrived and the group withdrew at around 12.30 a.m. a cache of improvised weapons – metal bars, a sledgehammer and wooden fence posts with nails – were found. Gardaí disputed the claims by a local protest leader, Willie Corduff, that he was injured in a separate incident after he had been hiding under the trailer of a lorry at the plant.

I knew from my own contacts in both the Gardaí and the PSNI that the protest groups had been attracting dissident republicans from both sides of the border. Some of those mentioned I knew well from the old days in Northern Ireland, but new, younger faces were appearing, too. The Corrib protests were becoming a rallying point for the dissident movement – a fresh recruiting ground, but the old guard remained at the forefront. A man who would later be questioned about the murders of the two soldiers in Antrim was arrested during a violent protest at the Corrib site in 2008. Another name that I knew well kept popping up with regard to the protests: a former member of PIRA who had been serving a 20-year sentence for a bombing but had been released under the Good Friday Agreement. A member of Éirígí, a newly formed republican group, he had been arrested at another protest at the site in 2008 but was not charged. Not everyone was opposed to the plant; in fact most people were very much in favour of it. It would employ close to 200 people when fully up and running. That was a lot of jobs in the west of Ireland, not to mention the knock-on effect it would have on the local economy. It was obvious that the dissident republican groups were hijacking the protests for their own benefit when Éirígí condemned what it termed the '26 county state' for allowing the Corrib plant to go ahead. So now I knew why a surveillance asset needed to be put in place.

I continued driving towards Castlebar. My target lay about ten miles north-west of the town. When I was sure I was well clear of the surveillance cameras that I knew dotted the border on the northern side, I stopped and pulled over. I popped the boot and opened the backpack, careful to put on a pair of latex gloves first. No way did I want my prints on this baby. The device was a camera but as modern and advanced as I had ever seen. It was a small periscope camera, designed to be buried beneath the ground with only a tiny lens that could be seen above ground. The battery was similar in design to the batteries I had used in the army, but it was much smaller, about the size of my fist, and I knew it was capable of powering the tiny camera for months. Transmission of the images would be via the SIM card that formed part of the camera. This was a very advanced piece of military-grade kit, and I now had a fair idea who I was working for. On the plus side, at least it wasn't a listening or tracking device, which would have involved a break-in or getting up close and personal with someone's vehicle. I switched on my GPS navigation unit and typed in the grid reference I had been given. I needed to know the exact place where the camera was to be buried. A drive-by would let me see if there were any houses nearby or if there was heavy traffic in the area. I needn't have worried; the location was as remote as you could imagine. There was nothing out here – a good place for a hide. I drove past the field without stopping, watching the GPS unit as I did so, noting the entrance to the field and the culvert. By now it was late evening. I would return after midnight and plant the device. In the meantime, I'd grab some grub and a few hours' sleep in the car.

I parked up about three miles from the field and made the rest of the way on foot across the broken ground that served as farmland in these parts. I had the backpack with me and a few tools I knew I would need. About 200 metres from the entrance to the field, I went to ground and kept watch on the area. There was no need for night-vision goggles or even binoculars that night; the sky was clear and the moon shone as bright as any midday sun. It was bloody freezing though, and the sweat I had worked up getting here was drying into me. I waited almost an hour and then moved towards the corner of the field diagonally across from the culvert. This would give me the best view of anyone approaching the culvert. I dropped to my knees and pulled the fold-up spade from the backpack and, as quietly as I could, I began digging a hole for the camera and battery pack. It didn't take long, but I needed to be sure that the view from the camera was what was required. I hooked up a small monitor to the camera and adjusted the lens until I had a perfect picture. The camera had both day and night functions which would allow it to capture anyone approaching. It was also infrared so could pick up the heat signatures as well. Satisfied, I filled in the hole until only the tiny lens was barely visible. Next, I surrounded it with rocks and brambles, still ensuring the lens had an uninterrupted view of the target. Job done! I made my way back to the car as quickly as possible and dialled Ted's number.

'Done. Everything OK your end?' I was counting on not having to go back in again.

'All good this end, mate. Cheers, I owe you one.'

And that was it. I leaned across to the glovebox and took out the envelope he had given me – €300. Ted had always been a tight bastard. It wouldn't have surprised me if he had snaffled half the fee for himself, but it didn't matter now.

In January 2010, Former UN Assistant Secretary General Denis Halliday launched an Afri petition supported by Archbishop Desmond Tutu calling for the suspension of work on Corrib, pending an independent investigation. In April of the following year, the Garda Ombudsman began an investigation after Gardaí were recorded laughing and joking about raping women they had arrested at the Corrib gas protest. In 2013, a German contractor, Lars Wagner, was killed during work on the Corrib gas underground tunnel. When work was completed in May 2015 on the Corrib gas tunnel, it was the longest of its type in Europe. It took almost ten years for final consent for the project to be granted by Minister for Energy Alex White, and the first gas was pumped ashore in 2015. The energy company Shell, which had started it all, would later sell its 45% stake in the Corrib gas field to a unit of Canada Pension Plan Investment Board (CPPIB) in a deal worth $947 million (€830 million). For me none of this mattered. All I had learned was that when it comes to British Intelligence, 'Once in, never out', still held true!

Chapter 21

Fallout – Keeping My Powder Dry

On 20 June 2018, almost a decade after the Anglo collapse, David Drumm was convicted on two counts of deceiving depositors and investors into believing that Anglo was healthier than it actually was at the height of the crisis. He was sentenced to six years in prison, although it is expected that he will only serve three and a half. He spent his first night in Dublin's Mountjoy Prison as prisoner number 102640. During his trial, Drumm had received free legal aid. The case, lasting eighty-seven days, had cost the taxpayer millions. For his part in the illegal loans to the ten developers, Drumm was given a suspended sentence of fifteen months. Tens of thousands of people in Ireland had lost their homes and their jobs. Taxes had sky-rocketed, public spending had plummeted and the next generation would be saddled with billions of euro of debt. Not only that, but many had paid a far higher price: unable to face the mountain of debt that was in front of them, the crash had driven many to take their own lives. Yet these people who had orchestrated the entire disaster were handed down sentences that could only be described as a disgrace. The whole thing was a farce. We are the laughing stock of the world.

On a personal level, I lost everything: my home, my business and my relationship with my partner, Steph. Steph had endured a lot during our time together and, in the end, it became too much for her. I am glad to say that since our split her life has blossomed. I had a small fortune owed to me, but there was no chance of getting it. I couldn't pay my bills or my employees. For years, I had watched the paranoia grow and the corruption that had plagued Ireland spread. Has anything really changed? No, I don't believe it has. Scandals of all sorts still raise their ugly heads. Bankers and developers continue to earn obscene amounts of money, and for the right amount in a brown envelope most things can be achieved in Ireland. I, like so many others, felt that I had failed. But information is my currency; it has been for most of my adult life, and a man with nothing left to lose and a world of secrets is a very dangerous man indeed. When I sat down to write this book, I'll admit there was some venom behind it, but not now. For me it has been a very therapeutic process. It has released some of the regret and sense of failure I had been experiencing since the crash. I have not revealed all my secrets, far from it. I have hundreds of hours of recordings and piles of documents that I am sifting through at my leisure. Many of those who now presume that the worst is over, that their secrets are safe and that they have gotten away without any real loss or consequences – beware! For as the saying goes: I am keeping my powder dry!